GIRL'S GUIDE TO GROWING UP

Navigating Puberty, Loving Your Body, Managing Emotions, Building Confidence, Staying Safe Online, Making Friends, Prioritizing Mental Health, and Planning Your Future!

Jane Mullen

ISBN: 978-1-962481-04-5

Copyright 2023.

Elk Point Press.

For questions,

please reach out to Connect@ElkPointPress.com

All Rights Reserved.

No part of this book may be reproduced or transmitted in any form or by any means, electronic or mechanical, including photocopying, recording, or by any other form without written permission from the publisher.

FREE BONUS

SCAN TO GET OUR NEXT BOOK FOR FREE!

TABLE OF CONTENTS

INTRODUCTION 1

CHAPTER ONE: WHAT'S HAPPENING TO ME? 5

   PHYSICAL CHANGES DURING PUBERTY 6

   GETTING YOUR PERIOD 8

   EMOTIONAL CHANGES DURING PUBERTY 14

CHAPTER TWO: LET'S TALK ABOUT PERIODS 17

   WHAT IS MENSTRAUTION? 18

   WHEN DOES MENSTRAUTION BEGIN? 19

   MANAGING MENSTRUATION 21

   MAINTAINING GOOD HYGIENE 23

   TRACKING PERIODS AND CYCLES 25

   MANAGING CRAMPS AND SYMPTOMS 27

CHAPTER THREE: TAKE CARE OF YOURSELF 29

   THE IMPORTANCE OF GOOD HYGIENE 30

   MENTAL HEALTH 32

   SKINCARE 36

   PREVENTING BODY ODOR 38

CHAPTER FOUR: EATING RIGHT AND STAYING ACTIVE ... 41

   IMPORTANCE OF A BALANCED DIET 42

   WAYS TO STAY FIT 45

   MAINTAINING A HEALTHY DIET 48

CHAPTER FIVE: FEEL GOOD INDSIDE AND OUT 53

    MANAGING EMOTIONS 54

    COPING WITH STRESS AND ANXIETY................................ 58

    BUILDING CONFIDENCE AND SELF-ESTEEM 62

CHAPTER SIX: STAYING SAFE AND SETTING BOUNDARIES
.... 65

    UNDERSTANDING PERSONAL BOUNDARIES 66

    STAYING SAFE OFFLINE 71

    STAYING SAFE ONLINE 73

    HANDLING UNCOMFORTABLE SITUATIONS..................... 75

CHAPTER SEVEN: BUILDING POSITIVE RELATIONSHIPS ... 77

    UNDERSTANDING HEALTHY RELATIONSHIPS................. 78

    FRIENDS AND FAMILY 82

    CONSENT IN RELATIONSHIPS... 85

CHAPTER EIGHT: TAKING CARE OF YOUR MENAL HEALTH
.... 87

    UNDERSTANDING MENTAL HEALTH 88

    SELF-CARE FOR MENTAL WELL-BEING.............................. 90

    ASKING FOR HELP WHEN NEEDED 94

CHAPTER NINE: LOVE YOURSELF FOR WHO YOU ARE 99

    UNDERSTANDING BODY IMAGE.. 100

    INCREASING BODY POSITIVITY 105

    REPAIRING A NEGATIVE BODY IMAGE............................. 108

CHAPTER TEN: DEALING WITH PEER PRESSURE 111

UNDERSTANDING PEER PRESSURE 112

RESISTING PEER PRESSURE... 115

BUILDING A SUPPORT SYSTEM 118

CHAPTER ELEVEN: PLANNING YOUR FUTURE 121

EDUCATION AND CAREER PLANNING 123

PLANNING YOUR FUTURE 128

BALANCING SCHOOL AND HOBBIES................................. 131

CONCLUSION.. 135

INTRODUCTION

Growing up can be a scary and overwhelming experience. As you get older, your body will go through a lot of changes, and your life will start to look different. Unlike in school, there is no clear path forward either; you won't get an award or certificate announcing that you have become an adult. The process looks different for everybody.

Growing up is a lifelong endeavor. It isn't like a storybook with a beginning, middle, or end. Becoming an adult is an ongoing story that will unfold over the course of many chapters throughout your life. There's no script to follow. The only thing you can do to prepare is to do your best and equip yourself with the right information.

It can be scary when you don't know what to expect. Don't worry, though! This book is written with you in mind, specifically for 8 to 12-year-old AFAB girls. If you aren't familiar with that term, it means "assigned female at birth." This means that if you were assigned "female at birth" or raised as a girl but do not identify as a girl (a trans boy), this book is for you too. Keep in mind that there are books that address the unique needs of trans boys specifically.

In this book, we will first address the physical changes that happen to your body during a process called *puberty*. Puberty is a journey that each person goes through in their early teen years. It is marked by a rush of hormones, causing distinct physical changes in your body and mind. Quite simply, puberty is a sign that you are growing into your adult body.

Additionally, we will explore the social changes that come with growing up. This will include a change in the dynamic between you and your family, friends, and peers. These ever-changing relationships are important to consider, because they have a significant impact on your life. However, we will also explore the importance of setting boundaries, avoiding peer pressure, and building – and maintaining – your self-esteem.

The later chapters will talk about the importance of personal hygiene and your physical and mental health. You will also learn a few tips for planning your future, balancing your hobbies with your education, and managing your time wisely.

It's normal to be nervous about growing up. Luckily, the more you understand something, the less scary it will seem. You're not alone in your experiences, and you deserve the right information, guidance, and respect.

Consider this book your general guide for growing up. You may finish it with more questions than you started with, and that's okay. You are lucky to live in a time where there is an abundance of information available. In fact, it's a good idea to share this book with a parent, guardian, or trusted adult. They may be able to answer additional questions that you may have.

4

CHAPTER ONE: WHAT'S HAPPENING TO ME?

There is more to growing up than driving a car, buying a house, or doing whatever you want whenever you want. One of the main stops along the journey to becoming an adult is puberty. Puberty is a process that happens in your early teens and signifies the point at which your body changes from that of a child to that of a young adult.

These physical and emotional changes can seem weird or even scary. However, knowing what exactly is going on will take much of the fear away.

Below, we'll go over a roadmap of the changes you can expect. You will start to understand *what's* happening in your body and *why* it's happening. In fact, you may notice that some of these things are happening already! However, keep in mind that everybody is different, and these changes will happen at different times for different people. With that in mind, don't worry if your peers seem to be growing up faster than you are!

Before we start, please note that the physical and mental changes listed apply to most kids and preteens who are Assigned-Female-at-Birth – AFAB, for short.

PHYSICAL CHANGES DURING PUBERTY

Puberty is triggered by a boost in the hormones flowing throughout your body, which in turn brings about a cascade of specific changes, such as growing taller. The main hormones involved in puberty are testosterone and estrogen. Everyone has a mix of both, but testosterone is mainly common in AMAB

("Assigned Male at Birth") people. Estrogen, on the other hand, is mainly found in AFAB people.

For an AFAB person, puberty usually begins between the ages of 8 and 13. You may have already started seeing some changes in your own body while waiting for others to kick in. The changes to look out for are:

- Breast development
- Increased body hair
- Oilier skin
- Change in body shape.
- Menstruation

Breast development is one of the earliest signs of puberty. This process will typically start around age 8 or 9, and you can tell because you will notice little "buds" growing around your nipples. Some girls begin developing breasts as early as age 7, while others start as late as age 13. Many factors, such as your genes, determine when your breasts will begin to develop.

For some girls, growing body hair is one of the first signs of puberty. You may notice hair sprouting up on different parts of your body, sometimes in the places where you least expect it! Hair will begin to grow on your legs and underarms, and a tuft of curly hair will grow between your hipline and vulva. You may notice hair on your belly button and upper thighs. While body hair is typically associated with AMAB people, it is natural for AFAB to have body hair, too. There is nothing wrong with letting your hair grow out!

However, there is one part of the puberty journey that every teen hates: pimples! When your face is dotted with pimples or blackheads, it's called acne. Acne is an extremely common skin condition that usually starts around age 12 and is caused by the oils on your skin clogging up your pores. This can be taken care of by washing your face once or twice a day. While there is no way to completely keep acne at bay, a regular cleaning routine is helpful and can help you feel good about yourself.

Remember, every teenager will get pimples, blackheads, or whiteheads. Acne is not a crisis; it's simply a natural part of puberty.

GETTING YOUR PERIOD

Growing into your adult body means gaining the ability to become pregnant and give birth. One of the ways puberty prepares your body for pregnancy and childbirth is by changing its shape. You'll probably notice your waist becoming proportionally narrower while your hips will tend to become wider.

In addition to these physical changes, you'll also start to get your period. This is one of the key milestones in an AFAB's puberty journey. This is the beginning of menstruation, also called menarche (*meh-nar-kee*), which is a sign that your body is ready to have a baby.

You'll likely get your period between the ages of 11 and 14, with 12 and a half being the average age. Some girls get their periods as early as eight years of age or as late as 15. Menarche generally occurs two or so years after your breasts develop. In the months leading up to your first period, you will notice small amounts of milky, white fluid coming from your vagina.

When you notice blood coming out of your vagina, this is called a period. However, this is not the same blood that runs through your veins. Period blood is a mix of blood, mucus, and tissue from the uterus. It can be light pink, red, or even brown. Typically, if you see a red spot in your underwear, this is a sign that you are getting your period!

After each menstrual cycle has concluded, a total of two to three tablespoons of period blood will have come out of your body. The bleeding should last around seven days, tapering off at the very end. We will soon get into the different ways to manage your period flow and prevent it from becoming a mess.

A few key parts of your body work together to make a period happen, but hormones are the main cause of them. These chemical messengers send signals to the other parts of your body that it's time to start the menstrual cycle. These other parts of your body are the:

- Pituitary gland
- Hormones
- Ovaries
- Uterus

The age when you get your first period is based on a number of factors. One of them is the age when your mother or birthing parent first got theirs.

Menstruation Symptoms:

When you are close to getting your period, there will be some signs and symptoms to look out for. Although these symptoms might be the result of something else happening in your body, they usually indicate that you are about to get your period.

The typical symptoms of your menstruation are:

- Abdominal Cramps
- Mood Swings
- Fatigue
- Bloating
- Acne

You may experience all or some of these symptoms a week before your period starts. Grouped together, these signs are known as "Premenstrual Syndrome," or PMS. PMS is completely normal and can be handled in different ways.

Other symptoms include hunger pangs and cravings, such as the urge to scarf down a cheeseburger or sugary drink. You may also have irregular bowels, whether that be diarrhea or constipation.

Hopefully, the symptoms that accompany menstruation don't scare you too much. It should make you feel better to know that every AFAB goes through the same thing, and there are plenty of things you can do to make yourself feel better before and during your period that doesn't involve eating an entire box of chocolates.

The Science Behind Menstruation:

To understand your period, you need to understand the complex science behind menstruation.

There are four main phases of the menstrual cycle:

- Menstruation
- Follicular Phase
- Ovulation
- Luteal phase

Menstruation is the first phase, and it is defined as the point when you get your period. You may have some of the symptoms described earlier in the chapter, such as cramps, mood swings, or bloating, which can show up before or during menstruation.

The menstruation and the follicular (*foh-li-cu-lar*) phase overlap, meaning that they take place at the same time. The follicular phase begins on the first day of your period. Your pituitary gland releases a hormone that tells your ovaries to produce follicles, which contain eggs or ova (the plural version of ovum.)

Shortly after, one of the eggs will mature while your body absorbs the rest. At this time, the lining of your uterus will get thicker, ready to nurture the mature egg. This process can last up to 16 days until the ovulation phase kicks in.

During ovulation (ah-vyooh-lay-shun), a mature egg is released from one of your ovaries. It leaves the ovary through your fallopian tube and eventually makes its way to the uterus. This is the phase when most AFAB people can get pregnant. During this phase, the mature egg waits for sperm to fertilize it.

The final phase is the luteal phase, which is when the lining of your uterus stays thick. If the mature egg doesn't get fertilized, the lining will shed, and the cycle will start again.

Managing Your Period

There are ways to manage your menstrual cycle while keeping yourself feeling healthy and mostly free of discomfort. For example, there are products you can use to prevent leaks that will allow you to go about your day as normal. There are a variety of products to choose from, depending on what you're comfortable with, your lifestyle, and your budget. What's even more exciting is that there are products made just for pre-teens and teens.

Creating a Period Kit

Now that you know that there are different products you can use to manage your menstrual flow, you can start assembling your own period kit. Whether you're still waiting to get your period or you've had it for a while, a period kit is a fun way to prepare yourself.

A period kit can be a box, bag, or purse containing some or all the items you need before and during your period. Some basic items may include:

- Tampons, pads, pantyliners (or any product of your choice)
- Wet wipes
- An over-the-counter pain reliever
- An extra pair of underwear (just in case!)

Ask a parent, guardian, or trusted adult to help you assemble your period pack and discuss what you need – or if you're missing anything. You can also have some fun picking out or even designing a small bag to contain those items. Keep this in your backpack or locker around your "time of the month."

Puberty Blockers

For some people, the changes that happen during puberty can be really hard or extremely uncomfortable. This is especially true for someone whose gender identity does not match the physical changes happening to their body.

In this instance, an AFAB who identifies as a boy (or who is trans) may need to delay or stop these changes from happening. They may receive puberty blockers, which will prevent them from getting their period.

If an AFAB person decides to live as the gender that they identify with when they get older, they will start gender-affirming hormone therapy (GAHT). For someone who is AFAB, this hormone therapy will allow their body to develop some of the same traits that an AMAB person develops.

Speaking with a Trusted Adult

Confiding in a trusted adult – such as a parent, guardian, relative, older sibling, or even a teacher – is something you should seriously consider during puberty. Even if you know the basic facts, you probably still have questions or want to better understand what you are feeling. A trusted adult can answer some of your questions and listen to what you have to say. If they don't have the answers you need, they can refer you to someone who does, such as a healthcare provider.

For example, you may have trouble managing the strong emotions that you feel during this time. Talking about them with someone who's already been through puberty can help you feel better, and they can probably give you tips on how to handle your mood swings.

EMOTIONAL CHANGES DURING PUBERTY

Your body *and* your mind will change during puberty. Perhaps you notice that you're getting a little more snippy than usual at your parent or guardian for not allowing you to stay up late on a weeknight or reacting more strongly when a classmate says something thoughtless.

You may also notice that you daydream about kissing your crush. Developing intense romantic feelings is an emotional change that happens when you become an adult. However, you may also not experience any romantic attractions at all during this time in your life.

You'll likely start to prefer the company of your friends over your family, and you will definitely care more about what your peers think. "Fitting in" might seem like the most important thing in the world to you. Peer pressure will be something to watch out for during this phase, as it can help shape you as a person – for better or for worse.

You may also find that not only do you want to become more independent from your family, but you are eager to try new things. However, keep in mind that the more independent you

14

are, the more responsibilities you'll have. It is good to learn how to take care of yourself, physically and mentally.

You will also become more aware of the world around you, developing strong opinions about the person you want to be or become. Your feelings will also get stronger, and your mood or feelings will change often. Remember, mood swings are normal! The only time you will need to worry is if your mood swings last for a long time and make it hard for you to do normal things, like getting out of bed or eating.

16

CHAPTER TWO: LET'S TALK ABOUT PERIODS

Although we touched on it earlier, it's time to learn more about one of the main indicators that you are starting puberty – your period! This chapter covers the most basic things you need to know about periods and the menstrual cycle, including when you should get your period and how to take care of it.

WHAT IS MENSTRAUTION?

Menstruation, also known as having your period, is one of the most important signs of puberty and will typically be the last to come. After your breasts have developed and hair has appeared on your body, your period should arrive.

The pituitary (*puh-too-uh-teh-ree*) gland in your brain tells the hormones in your body to do important things, like helping you grow into your adult body. A few years after you enter puberty, these hormones cause a lining to build up along the walls of your uterus.

You have two ovaries in your body, which will release an ovum (*oh-vum*) each month. The ovum, also called an egg, will attach to the lining of your uterus, waiting for sperm to fertilize it. The ovum and sperm have the "ingredients" needed to help a baby grow and develop, but one cannot create a baby without the other.

Like the egg, the lining along the uterus is important because it prepares your body for pregnancy. However, if the egg that is attached to the lining does not get fertilized, the lining will start to break down. When this happens, it will leave your body through your vagina, sweeping the unfertilized egg with it. This is your period or menstruation cycle.

WHEN DOES MENSTRAUTION BEGIN?

It's important to keep in mind that AFAB people will typically not get their periods until about 2 or 3 years after puberty has started. This means that your period can arrive as late as age 15. In addition, the entire period cycle itself is about 28 days (four weeks) long, which means you'll get your period about once a month; however, it can last either a few days longer or shorter, depending on many factors.

A few signs to keep in mind that indicate the arrival of your period include:

Cramps

You may feel discomfort in your lower abdomen, located below your belly. This happens because your uterus squeezes, "cramping" up, in order to get the lining off the sides of the wall.

Cramps are just a sign that your period flow is moving along as it should. The pain from cramps can sometimes feel worse during the first few days of your period, but thankfully, they should get less painful as you get older.

Mood Swings

You may also find that your mood is changing quite a bit right around the time you are about to get your period. Nothing is wrong with you; the culprit here is those pesky hormones!

Not only do hormones change your body and make it do certain things, but they can also affect the way you are feeling. This happens because hormone levels swing up and down throughout your period cycle.

Fatigue

If you are feeling more tired or less energetic around the time that you are supposed to get your period, this is normal, too. Fatigue is yet another unpleasant symptom of menstruation that is caused by hormones. In the same way that they affect your moods, hormones can also zap your energy levels as well.

Bloating

Your stomach may also feel swollen, and you may feel as if you have gained weight. This feeling is called bloating, and yet again, it's your hormones at work. Due to the rapidly changing levels of hormones, your body retains more salt and water, causing you to feel bloated.

Acne

Another symptom of menstruation is acne. Your hormone levels may drop right before your period starts, causing your glands to release more oil. Extra-oily skin causes clogged pores, which leads to breakouts. These same hormones can also cause your skin to become more inflamed.

MANAGING MENSTRUATION

Getting your period marks a major change in your life. However, this doesn't mean that you can't take charge of it. Managing your period is important to keep yourself healthy and feeling good.

Periods can be messy and inconvenient. Thankfully, there are things you can do to keep it under control so that you can live life normally. Below is a list of products you can use to help you manage your period.

Pads

Pads are items that you can use to soak up the period blood flowing out of your vagina. They are one of the cheapest and most readily available ways to manage your flow, as they can be bought in stores or online. Pads are made of absorbent material and are designed to attach to the inside of your underwear, soaking up blood for 3 to 4 hours (depending on the heaviness of your flow).

Some pads come with "wings," which are tabs of sticky plastic that you can fold under the edges of your underwear. These "wings" help keep the pad from moving around too much.

Disposable pads can only be used once and must be thrown away. Reusable pads are a good choice if you're worried about trash piling up or if you're worried about the environmental impact of disposable pads.

Tampons

Tampons are another common item used for absorbing your blood flow during your period. They absorb blood from inside your vagina and are meant to be thrown away after using them.

Tampons are made of an absorbent material that is compressed into a tube shape. This tube is inserted into your vagina using your fingers or an applicator. If inserted the right way, you shouldn't be able to feel them at all.

Similar to pads, tampons can be found in different sizes. There are slender tampons that are good for those just starting their period with a lighter flow and larger sizes for heavier days. Most packages come in an assortment of sizes.

There are also reusable tampons, and although they have been proven to be completely safe, you are more likely to get an infection from them.

Discs and Menstrual Cups

Menstrual discs and cups are other options if you feel that pads and tampons are too wasteful or uncomfortable.

These products catch blood during your period and can be worn for a longer time – up to 12 hours. Another cool thing is that they hold more blood than either pads or tampons. While both discs and cups both work the same way, there are some differences.

Menstrual discs are flat and small, making them a better choice for lighter flows, and are inserted further into your vagina than a cup. Menstrual cups have a curved cone shape with a soft nib at the end, which makes them easier to pull out.

Period Underwear

Period underwear is another great option to ensure you remain leak-proof during your period. This underwear can hold as much blood as two tampons for up to 12 hours, and one of these can be reused anywhere between 2 to 5 years.

Most types of period underwear are made with a material that traps your blood flow, usually a type of microfiber. Keep in mind that this type of underwear needs to be washed separately from your other clothes.

Hormonal Birth Control

Hormonal birth control is used to prevent pregnancy, and although the science is very complex, this pill basically causes your period to become lighter and shorter. Birth control is particularly helpful for AFAB people with irregular periods.

However, there are some unpleasant side effects of hormonal birth control. They can include nausea, mood changes, and headaches. Also, you cannot buy birth control at a store like you would any of the above products. You will need to see a doctor and get a prescription for this medication.

MAINTAINING GOOD HYGIENE

Taking care of your blood flow is only one part of maintaining good menstrual hygiene. Read ahead for some other good habits you can adopt that will keep you healthy and feeling your best.

Tip 1: Change your pads or tampons often.

Whether you decide to use pads or tampons, it is a good idea to follow the instructions on the package. For example, if you are using a disposable pad, you should change it every 3-4 hours. This will not only keep you comfortable, but it will also prevent the build-up of bacteria and reduce odor.

Keep in mind that you may have to change your pad more often during heavier flow days, especially to prevent blood from leaking onto your clothes.

Reusable pads should be changed as often as disposable ones. It's vital to make sure you are washing your reusable pads correctly.

Tip 2: Use mild soap and water.

Before and after changing your pad or tampon, it's important to wash your hands using mild soap and water. This will prevent bacteria from coming into contact with your vagina or genital area.

Keeping your genital area clean is also important. You can either use mild body wash and warm water to clean your vulva when taking a shower, or you can try flushable, hypo-allergenic wet wipes. Aim to clean your genital area at least twice a day, in the morning and evening.

Tip 3: Do not use strong soaps, sprays, or gels on your genital area.

You may not have realized it, but your vagina is a self-cleaning system. For this reason, there is no need to clean it with soap and water. More importantly, you should keep strong soaps, sprays, and gels away from your genital area, even if these items are sold as a "feminine hygiene" product. Although you may be tempted to use them to control odor during your period, using them is neither necessary nor a good idea.

Tip 4: Wear comfortable and breathable underwear.

Wearing underwear made with a breathable fabric, such as cotton, is a good way to keep your genital area free from infections and irritation all year round. However, wearing cotton underwear will especially come in handy when you have your period during the summer months. Typically, you can buy this underwear in bulk in a variety of sizes, patterns, and colors.

TRACKING PERIODS AND CYCLES

Tracking your period every month is a good idea for a couple of reasons. First, when you track your period, you will know when to expect it and can avoid being caught off-guard. Although you will not be able to predict the exact date, you can know the certain timeframe and ensure that you have all the products you need.

Tracking your period is also another way of making sure that you are healthy. Missing a period can be a sign that you need to see a doctor, so knowing which week you may get your period is a way to make sure that your body is working as it should. When you start seeing a gynecologist, they will usually ask you when you had your last period.

Calendar and Period Tracking Apps

You may already have everything you need to track your period, such as a calendar or pen and pencil. With this method, you can mark the day(s) when you are expecting your period and then jot down when it actually happens.

If you have access to a smartphone, laptop, or tablet, you can also download an app that allows you to track your period. Simply enter the beginning and end dates of your period. Some apps also let you keep track of other symptoms and note whether your flow is light, medium, or heavy.

Whether you decide to write down notes or enter information on an app, you can track your period by recording the following information:

- The first date of your period
- End date
- The total number of days

Keep in mind that the typical menstrual cycle is about 28 days. It's normal if you see that your cycle is shorter or longer by a couple of days, though.

Body Temperature

During the ovulation phase, your body temperature tends to rise. If an AFAB adult is trying to start a family and wants to get pregnant, tracking the menstrual cycle in conjunction with body temperature is helpful. While a rise in your body temperature can tell you if you are in the ovulation phase, it is not a sure sign.

MANAGING CRAMPS AND SYMPTOMS

As discussed earlier, menstrual bleeding is not the only sign that you are having your period. Cramps, bloating, and fatigue are other common symptoms, and they can be unpleasant, to say the least. If they're bad enough, they might even cause you to miss school and other activities. However, there are ways you can deal with these symptoms.

If your cramps, bloating, or fatigue get worse or make it hard for you to live a normal life, you should see a healthcare provider.

Drink Plenty of Water

Drinking plenty of water will keep you hydrated, which can help relieve the bloating you may feel before and during your period. Water can also help with some of the fatigue that you may experience. In general, it's a good idea to drink plenty of water each day, no matter what time of the month it is.

Eat healthy food.

It's not a surprise that you need healthy and nutritious food to nurture your growing body. This includes fruits, vegetables, and high-protein foods, such as fish and chicken. Yogurt and chocolate, in small doses, can be good for you as well.

Other "comfort" foods, such as salty, fatty, and sugary foods, are okay in smaller amounts. Keep in mind that eating too much of them can worsen some of your symptoms, especially bloating and fatigue.

Use a heating pad or hot water bottle.

A heated pad or hot water bottle can help you with cramps during your period. Simply hold the pad or water bottle against your abdomen for a short period of time. You can buy heating pads from your local drugstore or supermarket.

Medicine

Sometimes, over-the-counter pain relievers can help reduce cramps when they get intense. Ibuprofen is the most common medicine to take for cramps, and it is widely available at pharmacies and stores.

Birth Control

In addition to making your period flow lighter, birth control (or "the pill") can also reduce some of the other unpleasant symptoms. Birth control does this by reducing contractions in the uterus that cause cramps.

Get up and move around!

Exercising is one of the best things you can do for your body; it's great for anyone at any age. If you are already playing sports, dancing, running, or performing gymnastics, you are already on the right track!

However, if you're not, you should know that exercising is another way you can keep cramps and other unpleasant symptoms of menstruation at bay. Staying active releases hormones called "endorphins" that can make you feel happy and alleviate minor discomfort.

CHAPTER THREE: TAKE CARE OF YOURSELF

THE IMPORTANCE OF GOOD HYGIENE

Maintaining your personal hygiene is an important habit to develop, especially during puberty and as you enter adulthood. Not only will you keep yourself healthy, but it feels good to take care of yourself. Below are some general tips you can use when taking care of your personal hygiene.

Odor

Keeping yourself clean is one of the best ways to prevent body odor caused by bacteria, sweat, and other bodily secretions. The bad odor may keep you from feeling your best, especially at a point in your life when you are already self-conscious and worried about your image.

Germs

Regular hygiene can also prevent the spread of germs and bacteria, which can cause sickness, unsightly infections, and other health problems. Simple things, like washing your hands before eating or after using the bathroom, can help keep germs away. It's important to always cover your mouth when you cough or sneeze as well. Schools are one of the areas where germs spread very quickly, so be extra vigilant when in class.

Brushing your teeth is another important way of keeping yourself healthy. You should try to brush them at least twice a day, before going to bed and after getting up in the morning. Flossing, keeping your gums healthy, and regular visits to the dentist are also important.

Healthy Skin and Hair

Maintaining good hygiene also includes washing yourself regularly to remove oil, dirt, and dead skin cells. While it is important to feel good first, looking good can also help you in the long run.

Hormonal changes can wreak havoc on your skin, causing all kinds of uncomfortable skin conditions, including acne. There are ways to reduce and control these changes, though. For example, a nutritious diet and drinking plenty of water can help keep your hair and skin healthy.

Shaving your underarms or legs is not necessary for good hygiene. Many people who identify as women or girls prefer to shave their legs and underarms, but you will be just as clean and healthy if you don't.

Vaginal Health

While it's important to take care of every part of your body due to the significant changes happening to your reproductive system during puberty, vaginal health is extremely important. This includes maintaining the balance of vaginal flora and preventing infections. It is especially important to maintain your vaginal health as you start menstruating and start using products to manage your period.

Keep in mind that a light odor and small amounts of discharge are normal. However, if you notice a strong odor, itching, or more significant discharge, you should see a healthcare professional.

MENTAL HEALTH

Keeping your body clean is only one part of your personal hygiene. Taking care of your brain, making sure you feel just as good on the inside as you do on the outside, is just as important.

Since your hormones are in flux during puberty, you will experience a range of strong emotions, good and bad. Mood swings are normal, but there are many things you can do to help yourself feel better.

For example, it may feel impossible to learn how to manage your emotions. However, the first step towards this is accepting your emotions and getting comfortable with talking about how you feel. You can do this with a trusted adult, friend, or a mental health counselor who works with adolescents.

Talking about what you are feeling helps you feel better, as you are no longer bottling up your emotions. You may also want to creatively visualize or write about your emotions as another way of getting them off your chest.

Mental health can be especially tough during puberty, and it's not all because of hormones. The media and popular culture also contribute to feelings of anxiety and inferiority because they are constantly telling you what you should look like or think about.

There is a good chance you have access to social media, which is perfectly acceptable. However, keep in mind what content you are being exposed to. Not everything you see or hear is true, and it's important to develop an awareness of where your own thoughts are coming from. A healthy social media diet can help you maintain good mental health.

Factors That Impact Your Mental Health:

There are many factors that can affect your mental health, such as your habits, genetics, and peer pressure. However, one of the strongest factors that can affect your mental health is your body image.

Body image:

As your body is developing, you may not like what you see when you look in the mirror. While it's normal to want to look your best, you shouldn't be worrying too much about how you look. As long as you're getting the nutrition you need, sleeping enough, and getting exercise, that's all that matters.

If you are worried about your weight, speak to a healthcare professional. Sometimes, body image issues can make you feel depressed, leading to eating disorders and poor self-esteem. Bodies come in all shapes and sizes, and it's important to remember that body fat is completely normal.

However, for some people with gender dysphoria, their unique body image issues can be especially challenging. Not only are they worried about their appearance, but their body is developing in a way that does not match how they feel on the inside or how they identify. For example, an AFAB person who identifies as a boy may feel uncomfortable or stressed about developing breasts and other physical traits associated with becoming a woman.

Peer pressure:

Humans are social animals, meaning that we need relationships to thrive, such as the ones we have with friends and peers. However, it's important to maintain positive relationships and avoid peer pressure.

At this age, you are probably worried about fitting in and feeling accepted by your peers. The pressure you may feel to fit in is called "peer pressure," and it can be good or bad.

Positive peer pressure can help you grow and learn more about yourself or the world around you. You may be inclined to pick up new hobbies and interests, such as art, video games, or sports. Negative peer pressure, on the other hand, may force you to make decisions that are not good for you, such as having sex before you are ready.

Do not be afraid to say "no." Some of your peers may come from a different background from you and may think there's nothing wrong with what they are suggesting. Other peers may have the same values as you do and can help you stick up for your beliefs.

It's important to have compassion for yourself. You're on the journey to adulthood, learning about yourself and the world around you.

Academics and School:

Your schoolwork will also grow more challenging as you get older, and you'll likely get busier during your adolescent years. Your schedule will fill up with classes, after-school activities, social events, and other obligations. In fact, you may feel pressured to do well in every part of your life.

Time management is even a challenge for adults, but the earlier you learn how to do it, the better. Balancing your academics and school with everything else can be tough for kids and teens. It's important to eat well, drink water, get plenty of sleep, and speak to a trusted adult when you need to. Your physical and mental health should be a priority over schoolwork, no matter what.

Relationships:

Relationships are important in every phase of your life. These relationships include the ones with your parents or caregivers, other relatives, friends, peers, teachers, and anyone else you interact with on a regular basis.

During puberty, you may start having an interest in dating, which will introduce another type of relationship into your life. There are unique challenges that come with dating, and there are different things that can affect it, such as your preferences, values, and beliefs.

Having healthy relationships is a part of taking care of yourself. If you are having trouble in any of your relationships, they can start to negatively impact your mental health and overall well-being. Make sure you avoid interacting with anyone who makes you feel bad about yourself or who makes you feel unsafe.

Events:

Events in your life, in your community, or in the world also have a role to play in your mental health. Information will spread quickly because of today's technology and social media.

You may notice that bad news seems to constantly be popping up on your social media, leading you to believe that these terrifying events are happening all the time. It is important to accept your reaction to reading or hearing about these events, whether that is by writing down your thoughts or talking about them with a trusted adult. Whatever you decide to do, do not allow these events to impact you.

There are many things that may impact your mental health. To keep it intact, take care of yourself with a nutritious diet, exercise, writing, spending time with your friends, meditate, and speaking with someone you trust.

SKINCARE

It is *so* important to take care of your body during puberty. You will find that the tips below can be used for the rest of your life, ensuring that your body stays healthy well into adulthood.

Face

During puberty, your face might be plagued with acne and other skin problems. This is due to your raging hormone levels wreaking havoc on your skin. However, there are steps you can take to help keep it under control and make sure your skin feels – and looks – amazing.

One of the easiest things you can do is to gently wash your face with water at least twice a day. Ideally, you will want to also use a gentle face cleanser, which will wash away the dirt, oil, and bacteria that accumulate throughout the day without damaging your skin.

Another important tip is to wear sunscreen to protect your skin from the harmful rays of the sun. Sunburn can be an unpleasant experience, and prolonged exposure to the sun over the course of your life can also cause you to develop more serious conditions, such as skin cancer.

Body

However, there is more to personal hygiene than just keeping those zits and pimples at bay! Your growing body needs to be healthy, and good hygiene habits can help you reach that goal.

One of the most important things you can do to stay healthy is to eat a balanced and nutritious diet. This means that you are eating a good mix of fruits, vegetables, and proteins during the day. You can also enjoy a few treats here and there.

Don't worry; an occasional bag of potato chips or a scoop of ice cream will not cause you to become unhealthy. The main idea behind a balanced and nutritious diet is to give your body enough of the vitamins and minerals it needs to be healthy.

Your growing body also needs protein, which you can get from meats and dairy products, such as eggs, cheese, and yogurt. If you are not a meat-eater, or you do not consume any products that come from animals, you can eat tofu, nuts, chickpeas, and lentils. Taking supplements can also ensure that you have enough protein. No matter what your overall diet is, there are a variety of foods available to get the nutrition your developing body needs.

Drinking enough water throughout the day is also important and will keep your body healthy. Clean water is the healthiest drink for you and should be prioritized over sodas and juices. Another bonus point is that tap water is typically infused with fluoride, which can help keep your teeth strong. Staying hydrated also helps with symptoms of your period, such as bloating, cramps, and fatigue.

Exercise is another key ingredient for a healthy body. This does not mean that you need to do 100 jumping jacks or play sports every day. Going for a brief walk, dancing, swimming, and other activities can keep you healthy.

Also, never underestimate the power of sleep. Getting enough sleep each night has many benefits, such as improved energy and mood the next day. Sleep is vital, and it can also help you reduce stress. During puberty, you should do your best to get at least eight hours of sleep every night.

PREVENTING BODY ODOR

Most kids begin to develop body odor between the ages of 8 and 13. It happens at the same time as you begin to develop secondary sex characteristics, such as body hair and breasts. Your sweat glands will become more active during puberty, releasing chemicals that emit a strong odor when you sweat.

You cannot eliminate body odor, but you can control it. Here are a few tips you can follow to reduce body odor.

Showers

Taking a shower at least once a day can reduce your body odor. Consider taking one before bedtime, as you will feel refreshed and clean before getting into bed.

It is also a good idea to take a shower after playing sports, swimming, or any prolonged physical activity and after being outside during hot weather. This is because you sweat when you move around and use your muscles, leading to a more pungent body odor.

You may be especially worried about body odor during your period. Taking showers, using flushable wipes, and changing your pads, period underwear, or tampons can prevent odor during your period.

Deodorants

Deodorants or antiperspirants are handy items to have as part of your hygiene kit, and it's best to apply them right after taking a shower. You can buy these in various forms, such as roll-ons, sticks, creams, or sprays. Roll-ons and sticks may be easier to use and are more environmentally friendly than sprays. Some deodorants are also scent-free and hypoallergenic.

Clean Clothes

Changing your clothes, underwear, and socks is another way of reducing body odor. This also means keeping your clothes clean, so make sure you don't fall behind on laundry!

40

CHAPTER FOUR: EATING RIGHT AND STAYING ACTIVE

Eating a nutritious and balanced diet can help you stay healthy and feel good about yourself. Even if you don't eat meat, have food allergies, or stay away from certain food items because of your religious beliefs, you can still practice healthy eating.

Staying active is also important and is a great companion to eating well. In addition to being essential to your overall health, exercising can help you feel more in control of your body.

IMPORTANCE OF A BALANCED DIET

There are many reasons why eating a balanced diet is important, and doing so is important for anyone of any age. However, eating a healthy diet is especially important as a pre-teen since your body is still growing.

Nutrition

When your body goes through a growth spurt, there are nutrients that it needs to ensure it is able to support the growth. Protein, carbohydrates (or "carbs"), and fats are essential nutrients that supply your body with energy.

Your body also needs vitamins and minerals, and the best way to get those is through fruits, vegetables, protein sources (such as lean meats, fish, or tofu), and grains. It probably goes without saying at this point, but don't forget the water! Your body needs to stay hydrated, and water helps everything go down smoothly.

Energy

As we touched on before, a growing body needs more energy. During puberty, certain changes that are happening (such as starting your period) can drain your energy, making you feel fatigued. This means that you need to make sure that you boost your energy by eating the right kind of food.

In addition, the more you exercise or exert yourself physically, the more energy you will need. This is why it's so important to eat the right foods that will power your body.

Brain Function

The brain is one of the most important organs in your body, and just like the rest of your body, it needs nutrients to function well. In fact, studies show that a lack of nutrition can have a negative effect on brain development. This means that your brain will not be able to function the way it should, and you might have trouble doing certain tasks.

Healthy Weight

Worrying about the way your body looks, specifically how much you weigh, is common among pre-teens and teens. However, you can look and feel your best by maintaining a *healthy* weight.

If you are under or overweight, you may also start experiencing health problems that make it harder for you to live the life you want. A balanced and nutritious diet, coupled with exercise, can help you maintain a healthy weight.

Keep in mind that maintaining a healthy weight is important for *everyone*, not just pre-teens undergoing a growth spurt.

Growth

As you go through puberty, not only are the proportions of your body changing, but you're also growing in height. Healthy and nutritious food is necessary for growth, and inadequate nutrition can actually stunt your growth. For example, poor nutrition can delay breast growth and menstruation.

Skin and Hair

Another benefit of a nutritious diet, specifically one high in protein, is healthy skin and hair. Your nails – on both your fingers and toes – will also benefit from adequate nutrients, growing stronger and less brittle.

Immune System

Your immune system, one of the most important systems in your body, will also benefit from a good diet. Your immune system protects you every day from germs and other things that can make you sick, and like every important part of your body, your immune system needs nutrients, vitamins, and minerals to function well. These include:

- Iron
- Vitamin C
- Vitamin A
- Zinc

While a balanced and nutritious diet doesn't guarantee that you will never get sick, it helps your immune system work the way it should most of the time. If you do get sick, healthy foods can help you get better, along with plenty of rest.

WAYS TO
STAY FIT

Staying healthy requires you to do more than just eat healthy; you also need to exercise regularly. Now, this doesn't mean that you need to go to the gym or lift weights seven days a week. In fact, there are many fun and easy activities that can help you stay fit.

There are many ways to stay active, both alone and with your friends and family. Some of these you can do right in your home, while others will require you to go outside or get the right equipment.

One of the most important benefits of exercising is that it helps your body release hormones called endorphins. Endorphins are nicknamed the "happy hormone" because you feel good whenever they are released into your body.

Even if you have a disability or an injury that prohibits you from being physically active, there are still exercises that you can do.

Exercising in Your Bedroom:

Dancing

Staying fit can be as easy as playing your favorite song and dancing around to it! You can do this for a few minutes a day or a few times a week. It really depends on what you are feeling. An easy way to do this is to set an alarm on your phone to play a song with a good beat and just take a dance break whenever it goes off!

45

One of the best things about dancing is that you do it alone or with your friends, and it can even be done without music. Dancing is an excellent aerobic activity, which means that it's great for your heart and lungs!

Jumping Jacks

Jumping jacks are another fun and easy way to exercise. They can be done in the privacy of your own bedroom, and you can do as many as you wish. Start with a few and work your way up.

Yoga

Yoga is great for your balance, flexibility, focus, and overall physical fitness. You can do simple yoga poses in your home or any spot you find comfortable.

Yoga is also a great stress reliever. This is because it helps you focus and stay calm, as you need to utilize calming breathing techniques and exercises. You can watch videos online or ask someone to show you how to do simple yoga poses.

Fun and Easy Outdoor Exercises

While exercising in your home can be convenient and easy, you might feel more excited about exercising outdoors, especially in sunny weather! Sunshine converts a chemical in your skin into vitamin D, which your body needs to absorb calcium; you've probably already heard that calcium is essential for bone growth, and your bones are going to do a lot of growing during puberty.

Sunshine is also good for your immune system, and it boosts a chemical called serotonin in your brain, improving your overall mood. You'll want to remember to wear sunscreen if you are going to be out for a while, and remember to use one that's resistant to sweat!

Here are a few outdoor activities that you might enjoy:

Walking

Walking is a great way to stay fit, whether you go for a walk a few times a week or every day. However, the longer and more frequently you walk, the better it is for you. Walking is not only good for your muscles, bones, and heart, but it can also reduce stress and keep you calm. Walking in a park or in nature will have a positive impact on your overall mental health.

All you need is comfortable clothes, a good pair of shoes (or inserts), and an adult to accompany you. When you are old enough, you can walk on your own or with your friends.

Bike Riding

Learning to ride a bicycle is seen as a rite of passage for many kids, and it's a great way to stay active. Biking is good for your body and also serves as a reliable mode of transportation.

Biking is good for the environment and another fun activity you can do with your family and friends. Some studies have even shown that biking regularly can help your brain perform better in school.

Of course, keep in mind that bikes cost money. You also need to learn how to safely ride them and *always* wear protective gear.

Swimming

Swimming can be a very relaxing activity, and it's a great form of low-impact exercise as well. Learning how to swim can also be a life-saving skill to learn as well.

Swimming strengthens your muscles and keeps your heart healthy, like other aerobic exercises such as running and dancing. It can also help your skin stay hydrated and cool, which is important in the summer months.

MAINTAINING A HEALTHY DIET

At this point, you know that a balanced and nutritious diet, paired with regular exercise, is the key to staying healthy. The next step is to learn how you can eat healthy throughout the day and understand which foods will provide your body with the nutrition it needs.

Eat your fruits and veggies.

Fruits and vegetables provide your body with vitamin C, potassium, fiber, and many other essential nutrients. Nutritionists recommend that you eat five vegetables and two fruits a day, in any combination.

There are ways to include vegetables and fruits in all of your meals in varying amounts. For example, you can chop up fruit and mix it in with your favorite yogurt. You can also eat cooked or raw veggies with eggs, rice, and as a side to your favorite meals.

Eat your grains.

Pasta, quinoa, oats, and whole wheat bread can also supply your body with the energy it needs to keep growing. These grains are complex carbs that can be converted into an important fuel for your body, and they contain other important nutrients as well.

Make sure to always look for *whole* grains, as these are the best for you. They are not hard to find and come in the form of whole-grain pasta, whole-grain pizza, and whole-grain bread.

Proteins

Did you know that 50% of your body is made up of protein? Protein is a building block of your hair, skin, nails, and virtually every part of your body.

Your body needs a *lot* of protein in order to regain energy and function properly, as it also helps repair muscles and tissues. There are many high-protein foods to choose from, including some that you are probably familiar with, such as:

- Eggs
- Dairy products
- Meats
- Fish
- Beans
- Lentils

People who do not eat or use animal products, such as vegans and vegetarians, usually depend on beans, lentils, and other products for protein. Alternative to animal products include soy, seitan, seeds, and wild rice.

Also, if you are an athlete or play sports competitively, you'll probably need to eat more protein than those who aren't as physically active.

Eat three meals a day.

First and foremost, it's important to eat all of your meals and snacks at the table. At the very least, do not try to multitask while you eat, such as reading, watching TV, or playing on the phone. It is important to be focused and mindful of what you are eating.

You should eat 5 or 6 times a day, which includes meals and healthy snacks in between meals. Planning your own meals out can actually be fun, but remember to ask an adult to help you ensure that you are making the right choices and build a grocery list.

Limit sweets and caffeine.

Sugary foods may give you a spike in energy, but they won't make you feel better in the long run. Caffeine, an ingredient in many popular beverages, such as coffee and soda, can do the same thing. Caffeine keeps your body from absorbing calcium, which your growing bones need. There are a lot of healthy foods that will give you a more sustained energy level.

In addition, sugar can make your acne worse and is also bad for your teeth. No one is telling you to ditch refined sugar altogether, but it's important to be aware of how much you consume and try to keep it to a minimum. The same applies to fatty foods, such as burgers and fries. These foods may be delicious, but they contain "bad fats," which can lead to conditions like heart disease and diabetes (among others) and should not be eaten often.

Last but not least, drink lots of water!

By now, you probably feel like we're pounding this one in your brain; however, this tip is worth repeating because your body does need plenty of water. Whether you are feeling healthy or sick, have a headache, or are experiencing PMS, water helps things run smoothly.

You live in a time in which many types of beverages are available for you to choose from. While some claim to have all the nutrients and vitamins that your body needs, the truth is that water is the healthiest beverage you can drink.

Water helps all of the systems in your body, such as your immune and digestive systems, and helps your blood carry oxygen to cells in your body. Water allows your body to do all the work that is necessary for staying alive and healthy.

You should always drink water if you're thirsty – or even if you don't feel thirsty but haven't had any water in a while – especially every time you exercise. Your body simply cannot work well if you do not drink enough water, as dehydration can also keep your brain from functioning properly.

52

CHAPTER FIVE: FEEL GOOD INDSIDE AND OUT

Growing into a healthy adult is more than just getting your period and having a more developed body. Learning how to take care of yourself is equally, if not more, important, and one way of doing so is by looking after your mental health.

It's important to learn how to manage your emotions, cope with stress and anxiety, and build your self-esteem. Below are some key tips for taking care of your mental health.

MANAGING EMOTIONS

One of the hardest and most confusing parts of puberty is the emotional ups and downs that you will experience. One day, you may feel happy, while the next day brings feelings of sadness or anger; sometimes, this can even happen multiple times on the same day. Read on to learn about some things you can do to manage what you are feeling.

Sleep

Getting enough sleep at night is good for your body and mind. You'll feel better in the morning and throughout the day if you are refreshed from a good night's sleep.

To make sure you get enough sleep, keep up with some healthy habits. For example, eating a heavy meal, sweets, or anything containing caffeine right before bedtime is not a good idea. In addition, using your phone, tablet, or computer right before bed can also make it hard for you to sleep.

Lack of sleep can make you feel cranky and irritable. It can also make it hard for you to focus on school or concentrate on other activities that are important to you.

Exercise

Getting some exercise is key to taking care of yourself. Your growing body needs to stay strong and resilient, and fitting in some physical activity can also boost your mood.

You can exercise 10-15 minutes a day or for up to an hour. Some of the easiest exercises, all of which can be done at home, are:

- Walking
- Dancing
- Push-ups, squats, and sit-ups
- Jumping rope

Eat a balanced and nutritious diet.

Regular exercise and a balanced diet make a great pair! The foods you eat can affect your mood and how you feel about yourself. For example, eating a lot of refined sugar, simple carbs, and processed foods can cause unpleasant mood swings. If these foods make up a large portion of your diet, your overall health will decline, and you'll be more likely to develop a whole heap of health conditions down the road. Sugary and processed foods are difficult to digest and do not have enough vitamins and minerals to nourish your body, either.

In addition to contributing to the development of health conditions like obesity, diabetes, and heart disease, some studies have shown a link between a diet high in ultra-processed foods like sugary cereals and frozen meals to inflammation in the brain.

This inflammation can lead to an overall decline in brain function – including your mental health.

Eating a balanced diet consisting of vegetables, fruits, and proteins will give your brain the nutrients it needs to help you manage your moods and emotions better.

Journaling

Journaling can be a great outlet for your emotions and thoughts since your mental health is just as important as your physical health. There are many ways to journal, including writing, drawing, scrapbooking, and taking photos.

Journaling can not only help you develop an awareness of what is going on in your life, but it can encourage you to think differently about things. Getting your thoughts and feelings out of your brain and onto paper (or screen, as the case may be) helps you identify what exactly is bothering you, helping you process it more easily.

Limit social media and smartphones.

On average, kids aged 8-12 years old in America spend as much as 5 hours on a smartphone, tablet, or computer every day.

While smartphones and social media can provide a wealth of useful information, enabling you to do things like communicate with your friends and family faster, there are downsides. Studies show that spending more than 10 hours a week on social media can dampen your mood and negatively impact your self-esteem. In some cases, using social media can actually cause depression and anxiety.

Social media platforms provide us with a huge variety of content, including videos, images, and news. However, some of the content can affect the way you feel about yourself and the world around you. It also affects your mood and sleep schedule, making it harder for you to focus on what is important.

You can limit how often you check your social media accounts by focusing on activities that don't include staring at a screen or aimlessly scrolling for hours at a time.

Give yourself some space.

It's normal to want more privacy as you get older. This could mean having some space from your parents or even your friends. When you think about it, you probably spend much of your day being around others in school, at home, and in public places.

It's perfectly healthy to take some time to yourself to mentally charge or pursue some of your own interests and hobbies. This works out great if you have your own bedroom, and if you don't, speak to whomever you are sharing the room with and carve out some alone time. Noise-canceling headphones or earbuds can also help.

Do not compare yourself to your peers.

Your peers can be some of the most important people in your life during puberty. In fact, as you grow up, you probably want to spend more time with them than with your family. This also means that you care a lot about what your peers and friends think.

Forming relationships is a healthy and important part of life. Friends can inspire you to be your best while always being there for you, especially if you are going through a tough time. However, your peers can sometimes lead you in an unhealthy direction or make you feel bad about yourself. For example, you may not feel pretty or smart enough compared to them.

Fitting in can sometimes seem like the most important thing, but it's important to stay true to yourself and your values. Remember that if you are taking care of yourself and doing what feels right to you – with some guidance from a trusted adult and your guardians – there is no need to compare yourself with anyone else.

Be kind to yourself.

You are growing, adjusting, and learning. It's okay to make mistakes or have embarrassing moments; in fact, these are often the moments that teach us the most valuable lessons. At the end of the day, you should be kind to everyone – including yourself.

Don't be hard on yourself when you make mistakes or if things don't go as planned. It's okay to get frustrated when trying new things, but just remember you can learn from all of your experiences. In fact, learning from your mistakes and failures is a great way to help manage your emotions.

COPING WITH STRESS AND ANXIETY

As you grow up, your body and life will change. You'll have new responsibilities, harder classes, and more complex relationships, and at some point, you'll probably begin to feel more stress and anxiety. Remember, it's completely normal to feel stressed out about what is happening or might happen, like a big test coming up. It's also normal to feel anxiety about something bad happening, real or imagined.

However, if your stress or anxiety becomes too strong, it can be hard to focus on school or on other activities that are important, even things you enjoy. Stress and anxiety can also negatively impact your health, physically *and* mentally. These emotions can even lead to bad habits if left unchecked.

When you are anxious, your muscles get tense, your mouth may feel dry, and your heartbeat and breathing will become more rapid. This is your body's natural way of processing your worry and fear.

Read on to learn about some ways you can cope with stress and anxiety.

Eat healthy.

Eating a healthy and balanced diet is a good way to cope with anxiety and stress. This applies to everyone – adults, teens, and children.

While sugary and processed foods can increase your anxiety, this doesn't mean that you need to completely avoid sugar. There's nothing wrong with enjoying a scoop of ice cream or a doughnut occasionally. You just need to make sure that you drink plenty of water and eat foods that nourish your body with the vitamins, minerals, and proteins it needs.

Exercise.

Regular exercise, when paired with a healthy diet, is a great way to keep your growing body healthy. Not only is it a good part of self-care and personal hygiene, but it can also keep your stress and anxiety levels low. Physical activity also helps your body use up the hormones adrenaline and cortisol, which are released when you are stressed or anxious and releases endorphins, which act as the body's natural mood boosters.

Get enough sleep.

It shouldn't surprise you that lack of sleep can make your anxiety and stress worse. When you're tired, you have a harder time focusing and going about your day.

When you're tired, your body produces more cortisol in an attempt to give you an energy boost. However, this extra cortisol (sometimes called the "stress hormone") can also make you feel anxious.

To ensure you get enough sleep, make sure you stick to a bedtime routine during the week and practice healthy sleep habits. Doing the same activity before bed every night, such as solving sudoku puzzles or meditating, can help you train your brain to get ready to sleep. Refraining from using your bed for anything but sleep can also help if you have trouble falling asleep.

Do something enjoyable.

When you are feeling stressed or anxious, one of the best ways to handle it is to give yourself a "time out" and allow yourself to focus on an activity that brings you joy. For some people, this can mean doodling or listening to music. Even a short nap can be helpful.

Sometimes, the best thing to do is distract your mind from the things that are making you feel anxious or stressed out. What better way to do this than through an activity that you enjoy?

Take deep breaths.

Taking a deep, long breath can not only help you calm down but it will force you to focus on the present moment and clear your mind.

Since you breathe every moment of your life (your body does it automatically without you thinking about it, you might be wondering what's so special about doing this. For one, focusing on your breath can take your mind off things that seem overwhelming. You are giving yourself some relief.

Deep breaths can also be part of a simple routine called mindfulness. Pay attention to what is happening in the moment. Breathe in through your nose and then breathe out through your mouth slowly, counting to four each time.

Addressing Your Fears

It's important to keep in mind that not all stress or anxiety is bad. For example, being stressed about a ballet recital or a school play is not a bad thing. It means that these events are important to you, and you want to do well. In other words, these emotions can motivate you to do well. However, if you fail to deal with these feelings, they can strengthen and become unhealthy.

Everyone is afraid of something, even things that do not directly affect them. For example, you may worry about a natural disaster or other event that you heard about on the news. Your fears can make you anxious and stressed.

Try a few of the following techniques to help ease your mind:

- Speak with a trusted adult.
- Acknowledge your fears.
- Gather information about the things that worry you (after all, the more you understand something, the better you will feel)

It is impossible to live completely free of fear and worries, but you have to understand what you are feeling and why you are feeling it before you can address it and move on.

BUILDING CONFIDENCE AND SELF-ESTEEM

Taking care of your body is just one part of growing into a healthy and happy adult. You will encounter challenges and adversity throughout puberty, and they don't stop there. Adulthood will have its own set of problems.

Learning how to cope with stress and handle challenges are important life skills. Building your confidence and self-esteem will make these a lot easier. Let's take a look at a few different ways you can go about building up your confidence.

Focus on being healthy.

Caring about your outward appearance is normal; you are unique, and most people will identify you by the way you look. Personal hygiene can help you feel good about the way you look. However, while paying attention to your appearance is normal, you should focus on being healthy. After all, nothing beats that healthy glow!

Clear skin and shiny hair are just two ways being healthy can impact your appearance. Staying healthy means getting at least eight hours of sleep every night, exercising, eating a balanced and nutritious diet, and caring for your mental health. Sometimes, you might need the help of a healthcare professional to accomplish this, and that's okay.

Focus on the effort and progress, not just the reward.

When you ace a test or win an award, it can feel amazing! It's great to be recognized for your effort, hard work, and talent. However, it's important to remember that you won't get a prize for every hard thing you do.

Sometimes, you may fail and exclaim to yourself, "I can't do it!" When this happens, remember that exercising your brain is just as important as exercising your body. This means trying new things and being okay if you aren't good at them at first. The process and progress you make is just as important as the result, not to mention that determination and persistence are qualities that will help you in almost every aspect of life.

Explore your interests.

One of the most exciting parts of growing up is trying new things. You are becoming your own person, and this means developing hobbies and interests of your own.

Joining after-school clubs and forming hobby groups are two ways you can do this. Even if you are limited by finances, disability, or resources, your school or community organizations probably offer opportunities that you can explore.

Stand up for yourself and what you believe in.

Standing up for yourself might be hard, but it's one of the most important things you can learn how to do. On top of this, peer pressure usually makes standing up for yourself even harder, but you should not give up.

Remember, relationships are an important part of life, and your friends can influence you in many ways. However, their influence can be good or bad, which is why it is important to stand up for yourself. You should not feel pressured to do anything that makes you feel uncomfortable or causes physical or mental harm.

CHAPTER SIX: STAYING SAFE AND SETTING BOUNDARIES

Staying safe and setting boundaries are important parts of being healthy and happy. Not only can boundaries help you maintain healthy relationships, but they can also help you walk away from unhealthy ones.

UNDERSTANDING PERSONAL BOUNDARIES

In order to set boundaries, it is important to understand what they are, why they are important, and how to communicate them. Below is an overview of what it means to have personal boundaries and, more importantly, how to enforce them. If you have any questions, you should speak with a trusted adult or reach out to your school for more information and resources.

What are personal boundaries?

You probably first heard the word "boundary" in class when learning about shapes, countries, or states. Boundaries apply to physical things, like land or property. They are used to mark one thing from another, protecting whatever they contain. For example, fences and gates are boundaries for a house or a piece of land.

In the same way that physical boundaries protect a piece of land, personal boundaries protect an individual. Setting boundaries is a way to communicate how you expect to be treated while also ensuring that you keep yourself safe. Think about it as setting up invisible fences between you and other people, including family, friends, peers, and strangers.

When you were younger, it was probably harder to set and insist on your boundaries because the adults in your life had more of a say. However, everyone is entitled to set boundaries, including children.

Types of Personal Boundaries:

Just as there are different types of physical boundaries, such as fences, sidewalks, and doors, there are also different types of personal boundaries. These include:

- Physical boundaries

- Emotional boundaries

- Mental boundaries

All of these boundaries are equally important, and together, they make up your personal space.

Physical Boundaries

Physical boundaries pertain to your body and everything that belongs to you, such as your clothes, toys, and journal. You may not want anyone to take or touch your stuff without asking you first.

Another important physical boundary applies to your body. No one should touch you or any part of your body without your consent. You have the right to say "no." For example, you may not feel comfortable when family members scoop you up or give you a kiss when you don't want them to. Many people think that this behavior from adults or other kids is okay, but if you do not feel comfortable, you have the right to say "no." At the very least, they should ask you first.

Unwanted physical contact can feel uncomfortable, and you have the right to express that discomfort! Everyone is in charge of their own bodies, and "no" is a complete sentence.

Examples of Physical Boundaries May Include:

- Asking a relative to ask you for permission to kiss or hug you.

- Telling other kids that they need to ask you before they touch any of your things.

- Asking your parent or guardian not to touch or open your diary.

- Being comfortable saying "no" when another kid asks to play with you when you do not want to

Emotional Boundaries

Emotional boundaries are trickier to describe and not as obvious as physical ones. So, what are emotional boundaries, and how do you set them?

You can create a boundary or invisible space around your feelings by becoming aware of your emotions and acknowledging them. Using "I feel..." statements can be helpful in communicating with others.

Another way to understand emotional boundaries is to think about how you want to be treated. Do you hate it when your friends tease you about your freckles or some other part of your appearance? Does it make you sad when your parents or guardian yells at you?

Emotional boundaries are a way for you to let others know when you are feeling hurt or scared. You should let others know if what they are saying or doing upsets you, especially if they are doing it with the intention of making you feel bad.

Examples of Emotional Boundaries May Include:

- Sharing how you feel (but you can decide when and what to share)

- Asking for privacy or alone time (being around others can get overwhelming, and sometimes you just need to step away and spend some time by yourself)

- Asking your friends to stop making fun of you (especially if they are making fun of how you look, dress, talk, or your cultural and religious background)

- Letting another person know that you want to be left alone (sometimes you don't even know why you are upset)

- Asking someone to stop saying mean or hurtful things (to you or others)

Mental Boundaries:

Sometimes, you can cross your own boundaries, and this usually happens when you talk to or about yourself in a negative way. There's nothing wrong with thinking about how you can be better at something or what you've done wrong. However, a constant stream of negative thoughts about yourself – whether it's about your appearance, thinking that you aren't smart enough, or something else – shows that you do not respect yourself or value who you are.

If you think "no one likes me" or "I am so stupid," you will only get in the way of your own happiness. Therefore, a good way to set a mental boundary is to stop attacking yourself as a person. Instead, focus on what you *do* like and how you can improve. Adopt healthy habits and express your thoughts and feelings rather than comparing yourself to others.

Examples of Mental Boundaries May Include:

- Deciding what kinds of media to watch (there's content that is not suitable for kids anyway, but there may be some things in particular that bother you, such as scary movies)

- Refusing to engage in negative self-talk (such as telling yourself that you are ugly, stupid, or that no one likes you)

- Asking your parent or guardian if you can get involved in some household decisions (that way, you can feel more in control of what happens to you)

Why are personal boundaries important?

Physical, emotional, and mental boundaries are important for your overall health. Setting boundaries can not only help you grow but can also help you handle challenging situations.

Personal boundaries are necessary for creating and nurturing healthy relationships. Someone who hurts you, physically or emotionally, is crossing one of your personal boundaries. Sometimes, they do it by mistake because they do not know what your boundaries are. In some cases, they just need to be told what your boundaries are, and they will respect them going forward.

However, there will also be times when somebody decides to violate your boundary repeatedly. In this case, you may need someone else, like a trusted adult, to step in and help you set your personal boundaries.

Personal boundaries are important for adults *and* kids, but to get better at setting and maintaining your boundaries, you should start early. Some adults have a hard time setting boundaries because they weren't taught how to do it when they were kids.

Kids also have a right to set personal boundaries. After all, a kid is still a person who needs to feel comfortable communicating what they want and need from others. Everyone deserves to be treated with respect.

STAYING SAFE OFFLINE

Contact Information

Every child should know their address and the phone numbers of their parents or guardians. If you have trouble memorizing this information, write it down on a card and keep it in your pocket, school bag, or another easily accessible location. Don't rely solely on your phone! Phones can break, run out of battery life, or get lost when you need them most.

This information is helpful if you get lost or feel that you are in danger. An adult can help you contact your parents or guardians if needed. If you have a smartphone, make sure you can find this information quickly.

If you're going on a school trip or to a sleepover, make sure that your hosts know how to reach your parent or guardian in case of an emergency.

Tell your parent or guardian where you are going.

Always tell your parent or guardian where you are going when you leave the house. If you're visiting a friend, be sure to tell the hosts (in most cases, your friend's parent or guardian) how to get in touch with your parents.

If you are going to a pool, park, or playground, make sure you have your parent's or guardian's contact information with you. It may be a better idea to have your parent/guardian or another trusted adult chaperone you.

Don't follow strangers.

You should never follow a stranger, even if they say that they were sent by your parent to get you. Stay where you are and call out for help.

Another good idea is to come up with a "password" that only you and your parent know. If they send someone you haven't met (or even someone you have met but don't know well) and that person knows the password (and the name and address of your parent/guardian), then it's okay for you to leave with that person.

Assert your personal boundaries.

If someone is pushing or violating one of your personal boundaries, let them know. In most cases, they will listen and hopefully remember. If they don't, reach out to a trusted adult to help you.

Tell someone if you are in danger.

If something doesn't seem right and you feel like you are in danger, let a trusted adult know. Trust your instincts if something feels wrong and remember it's okay to say "no!".

STAYING SAFE ONLINE

The internet is a great source of information and an easy way to connect with other kids. However, you should keep in mind that there are as many dangers online as there are offline. If you use the internet a lot and you have access to a smartphone, you need to know how to keep yourself safe.

Think before you send.

Do not share any personal information online. This includes your address, where you go to school, and any other private information about yourself. There is no good reason why someone should be asking a kid for that information online.

If you have access to a smartphone and you text your friends, think about what you send. Some content is inappropriate, such as texts with bad language and naked photos. You should not be sending or receiving those from anyone.

Do not talk to strangers.

If you use certain apps or play games online, you may receive messages from strangers. It's best to ignore them; the only messages you should pay attention to are the ones from your friends.

Make sure you know your friends' usernames and can confirm it is them. It's also helpful to know the privacy settings of the apps you use. In some cases, you can keep people you don't know from contacting you.

Learn how to use privacy settings or use parental controls.

Make sure you go over the privacy settings for each of your apps. Your parent or guardian can even install apps that protect you from inappropriate online content. Other apps allow parents to set different controls, which can prevent access to apps that are not suitable for kids.

Privacy is important for everyone, but it is a good idea for your parent or guardian to supervise your internet access and use.

Report Cyberbullying

When a person uses the cell phone or the internet to send mean texts or images to someone else, it is called cyberbullying. The cyberbully could be someone you know or a stranger.

If someone is bullying you online, let a trusted adult know what is happening. Again, you should follow your instincts; if someone is making you feel uncomfortable, scared, or unsafe online, you will need a trusted adult to step in and help.

If you find out that the cyberbully is someone you know, tell your parent or guardian so that they can speak with the parents. One of the first things you can do is step away from the computer or whatever device you are using.

HANDLING UNCOMFORTABLE SITUATIONS

It is a sad fact that you may find yourself in a situation that makes you feel uncomfortable or even threatened. You should pay attention and acknowledge whenever someone violates one of your personal boundaries. These situations can be especially scary for a kid, but if you do find yourself in an uncomfortable situation, here are a couple of things you can do.

Speak up.

The first thing you should do is speak up. Let the person know that you are not comfortable with what is happening. Whether it's something they're doing or saying, you should let them know how you feel.

This may seem simple, but it can be hard to speak up. You might be afraid of how the person may react. If the person is an adult, then it may feel weird to stand up to them. However, the bottom line is that you deserve respect, and no one should violate your boundaries.

Get help.

If the cyberbully does not listen when you speak up or repeats the behavior, you should speak to a trusted adult. Everyone needs help occasionally, and it's hard to solve certain problems on your own. Sometimes, you need an adult to step in and help you, and that's okay.

CHAPTER SEVEN: BUILDING POSITIVE RELATIONSHIPS

One of the most important skills you can learn is how to build positive and healthy relationships. These relationships include the ones you have with family, friends, and peers. As you get older, these relationships can also start to include the people you work with.

This chapter is about building positive relationships with family and friends. To be able to do that well, it is important to understand the building blocks of a healthy relationship.

UNDERSTANDING HEALTHY RELATIONSHIPS

Take a moment to think about what makes a good house. You need a strong foundation and solid building materials, right? In the same way, relationships need foundations that keep them healthy and strong. Houses also need pillars and frames, and these can be compared to other aspects of the different relationships in your life, too.

Respect

What does respect look like in a healthy relationship? Respect means that you and the other person are kind to each other despite any differences between you. Even when you are angry or have a disagreement, you take turns listening and speaking calmly. It's okay to disagree, but it's not okay to call each other nasty names or make fun of each other.

Respect also means that you and the other person in the relationship avoid forcing each other to do what you want. Now, you may be thinking to yourself, "My parent(s) try to tell me what to do all the time!" This is because a good parent or guardian wants to guide you to do the right things, even if you do not want to do those things. Listening is a good idea if it is not harming you, especially if they are trying to help.

Good friends can also help you become a better person, and you can help them, too! Just remember that it's not a healthy relationship if the other person is causing you to do poorly at school or behave disrespectfully towards others.

If someone does not honor your personal boundaries, harms you, or makes you feel bad about yourself, then they are not respecting you.

Trust

Imagine that you tell your friend a secret, and you ask them not to tell anyone else, but your friend tells other kids your secret anyway. You would feel upset or angry with your friend, right? If your friend does this often, then you will start to feel as if you cannot trust them.

If you trust someone, you know that they will say what they mean and do what they promise. You may also feel that they would not do anything to harm you, and you can count on them to help you.

As you get older, the adults in your life will begin to put more trust in you. They will trust you to get things done, do your chores, and tell the truth.

Communication

Imagine you're playing a game with your friends, but no one explains the rules. It would be confusing for a friend who has never played it before, right? They might be able to get the rules while watching everyone play, but it would be easier if someone *told* them.

Now, imagine that your friend or parent/guardian does something that bothers you. They may be able to tell that you are upset by your body language, but there's no guarantee of that.

Even if they can tell that you're upset, they may not know *why*. That's why it's probably easier to tell your friend or parent/guardian that you are upset or not feeling okay and what made you feel that way. When people share their feelings or talk about what their boundaries are, they are communicating. Communication is a pillar of a healthy relationship, and it is important in every other aspect of your life as well.

There is more to good communication than just sharing how you feel or talking about your rules and boundaries, though. Being a good listener is also an important part of good communication. This is called active listening, and it means that you pay close attention to what the other person is saying. Active listening includes:

- Making eye contact with the other person
- Avoiding distractions by doing things like putting away your phone or shutting off the TV
- Responding to what is said, but *only* after the other person has finished talking.

These are just a few things you can do to show that you are paying attention (and ensure that you are!) If you do this, it will encourage the other person to listen actively when you are talking as well.

Kindness

You may think that being kind just means being nice, but they are actually quite different. For example, saying "thank you' when someone does something for you is a way of being nice. Inviting someone to your birthday party is another way of being nice. When you are nice to someone, both you and the other person will feel good. However, being nice is ultimately about pleasing someone and making them feel good while being kind shows that you actually care about them.

Being kind can be harder. Kindness is intentional and involves respect and consideration. For example, if one of your friends runs and then falls into a puddle of mud in front of everyone, it may seem funny. You may feel like laughing with everyone else, but the right thing to do is to help them up, give them a hug (with their permission), and ask them if they are okay.

Now, imagine if you were the one who fell. How would it feel if everyone, even your friend, laughed at you? If you aren't sure what to do, ask yourself, "How would I feel if that happened to me?"

Another aspect of being kind is telling the truth. It's the right thing to do, even if it sometimes doesn't feel nice. However, being kind is about comforting, supporting, and telling the truth in order to help the other person. Even a small act of kindness can help someone.

Cooperation

Cooperation means working together with another person to make something happen. Wouldn't it be hard to play a game if no one followed the same set of rules? When you have a playdate or visit with a friend, you share ideas about what you want to do. You think of an activity or a game and then agree on what it is and how to do it. For example, you may want to draw and color, but your friend wants to play school. If you want to play together, you will have to find an activity that you both want to do. This is an example of cooperation.

When you interact with other people, you will not always get what you want. Sometimes, you go along with someone else's plan, and sometimes they go along with yours. In a healthy relationship, people cooperate. You share ideas and take turns deciding on an activity or on how to do it. It is not healthy if one person makes all the decisions.

FRIENDS AND FAMILY

Family and friends are likely the most important people in your life. Because of this, fostering positive relationships with your family and friends is necessary for growing up into a healthy and happy adult. However, keep in mind the following characteristics that define a positive relationship, including:

- Showing respect
- Being supportive
- Listening actively
- Showing gratitude

- Embracing quality time

Respect

Respect is one of the most important qualities you can develop for a positive relationship. It means telling the truth, sharing feelings, and honoring boundaries. For example, you show your parents/guardians respect by listening to what they say. You know that they want to guide you to make the right choices, and it would be wise to follow their advice.

Accepting another person as they are, as long as they do not harm you, is another way of showing respect.

You should be treated with respect as well. Your family and friends should respect you by honoring your boundaries and supporting you to make good and healthy choices.

Being Supportive

People in positive, healthy relationships help each other through good and bad times. You can help someone in various ways, such as listening, comforting, or just being there for them.

Being supportive is a way of helping someone, too. Fostering positive relationships with your parents or guardians means that they support you when you experience challenges or are trying to achieve a goal.

As you get older, your life will become more complex. It can feel overwhelming when you are dealing with school, responsibilities at home, or break-ups. Your friends and family can support you by giving you some advice or encouraging you to do your best.

Family and friends can also support you by helping you find a counselor or a professional who can help you with your mental health.

Listening

Listening without interrupting another person during a conversation is key to building positive relationships. For example, your parent/guardian can show that they are listening to you by giving you their full attention. This means no phone or TV in the background, sustained eye contact, and follow-up questions when you are done speaking. This is that active listening we discussed earlier, and it's another way of supporting someone and showing that you care.

Showing Gratitude

When someone does a good deed for you, it is nice to say "thank you" or do something else to show that you appreciate what they have done. This is also called showing gratitude. Appreciating the good things, big and small, that your family and friends do for you is an important pillar of a healthy relationship.

Keep in mind that gratitude does not mean you need to list out every good thing that was ever done for you. It just means that when you are feeling bad or upset, you can think about the good things in your life and the people who make you happy.

Try thinking about the things that you are thankful for every day before going to bed. They can be anything, big or small, such as getting an "A" on a spelling test or going for ice cream with your best friend.

Listing what you are grateful for, whether you say it out loud or write it down, can boost your mood and remind you of the things that make you smile.

Embracing Quality Time

Carving out quality time with one another is just as important to a healthy relationship as the other things we've mentioned. Spending quality time allows you to connect with your family members or friends by doing an activity together without distractions, such as talking, going on a walk, or eating a meal.

While it can be challenging to establish quality time with family members and friends, especially if you're busy with school, homework, or appointments, it's important to try. For example, you and your family can plan to have dinner together a few times a week without TV, phones, or other distractions.

You should also make sure to have fun with your family and friends. Find activities that you enjoy doing together and schedule times to do them. Doing these fun and interesting activities with the people in your life can help you feel more connected to them.

CONSENT IN RELATIONSHIPS

Consent is an important part of healthy and positive relationships, as it helps you set boundaries and demand respect. If you think about a tree, you can imagine consent as being the trunk and your personal boundaries as the branches and leaves.

Giving consent means agreeing to something or allowing someone to do something. For example, when a family member or friend asks you if they can give you a hug, they are asking for your consent. If you do not consent to a hug, they shouldn't try to hug you because you did not agree to let them.

Giving or denying consent allows you to make choices about your own body or life. It also keeps you safe and healthy because no one should pressure you to do things that can harm you or make you feel uncomfortable. Another example has to do with social media. If you do not want your family members or friends to post pictures of you on social media, you can tell them that you do not give consent.

Before you consent to something that you are unsure about, you can ask yourself:

- "Am comfortable doing that?
- "Does it make me feel unsafe?"
- "Do I understand what they are asking?"
- "Do I trust and feel safe with this person?"

If you do not feel comfortable in a situation, ask a trusted adult to get involved. They can help you keep your boundaries and feel safe while working with you to come up with new ones.

CHAPTER EIGHT: TAKING CARE OF YOUR MENAL HEALTH

Taking care of your mental health is as important as caring for your body. It's hard to feel confident, grow, and live out your dreams if you aren't healthy, inside and out.

UNDERSTANDING MENTAL HEALTH

To take care of your mental health, you need to understand what it is and why it's so important. There is more to growing up than just the physical changes you can see and feel happening to your body. You also need to understand what is going on in your mind and how to take care of yourself.

The Importance of Mental Health

Your mental health is just as important as your physical health. To keep your body healthy, eating nutritious foods and getting regular exercise are good practices. So what do you need to do to keep your mind healthy?

Feeling lonely, sad, or anxious at times is normal. However, if you are often confronted with those negative emotions, it can be hard for you to focus on school, or even activities that you enjoy. You may find it hard to sleep or take care of yourself.

If you have good mental health, then more often than not, you have positive feelings and thoughts. It's normal to feel sad when a pet dies or when you have a fight with your friend, just as it's normal to be anxious about a test. However, if you have sad and anxious thoughts most of the time, it could be a sign that something is wrong. Read on to learn about ways in which you can cope with negative thoughts and feelings.

Emotions

Emotions are an integral part of mental health. Your feelings can influence how you see the world around you and the way you behave.

By themselves, emotions are neither good nor bad, but it can be hard to stay focused when you are feeling sad, angry, or anxious. If these feelings become too strong or last longer than usual, you may want to ask a trusted adult to help you. If you're only feeling these "bad" emotions sometimes, though, there are steps you can take to help you feel better.

Don't ignore or try to "put away" your feelings, even the bad ones. Acknowledge them and say to yourself "I feel very sad" or "I feel nervous right now." One of the best things you can do is give a name or label to your emotions.

When you're feeling sad or angry, you may not feel like talking. Giving yourself space and asking everyone to leave you alone can help you calm down. Sometimes, all you need to do is take some time to write, draw, or engage in another calming activity.

These are just some general tips on how to manage your emotions. There are many additional practices that you can follow to take care of your mental well-being.

SELF-CARE FOR MENTAL WELL-BEING

Taking care of your mental health begins with understanding your emotions and what affects your mood and thoughts. There are some skills and activities you can do to help yourself and the adults in your life during times when you're experiencing challenging emotions and thoughts.

Some of these are practices you can do on your own, but you may want to ask an adult to help you decide what practices are best and how to start including them in your routines.

Coping Skills

An important part of taking care of your mental well-being is learning coping skills. These are strategies that will help you navigate difficult experiences. It's important to remember that not every moment of your life will be filled with fun, peace, and happiness. Difficult experiences and challenges are a natural part of life.

Learning effective and healthy coping skills can make you stronger and more confident. For example, it's okay to feel angry if you fight with your friend or if something doesn't go your way, but you need to deal with the feeling rather than ignore it. Giving yourself the space and time to feel and process the negative emotions will often help you work through them.

You can also learn from failure or difficult experiences. If you lose a dance competition, you can keep practicing and try again next year. If your family lost a pet, give yourself time to grieve and keep memories of your beloved animal.

If it feels like your "big emotions" are too much to handle, speak to a trusted adult, a school counselor, or anyone else you feel comfortable with. Sometimes, just talking things out can help you feel better.

Verbalizing Emotions

As we noted above, talking about what you are feeling can help you feel better. Here are easy steps that you can follow when you want to verbalize or talk about your emotions:

- Recognize
- Identify
- Speak

Recognize what you are feeling. Whether you are feeling lonely, sad, angry, or anxious, it's important to acknowledge your emotion and get it out in the open.

Identifying what you are feeling is giving a name or label to it. While it doesn't have to be completely accurate, the idea is to communicate what you are feeling.

Speaking about what you are feeling is the next step. You can write in your journal or doodle, but if that doesn't make you feel better, speak to a trusted adult. They can help you understand what you are feeling and why you are feeling it, while guiding you in the right direction. Speaking about your feelings can help others understand what you need and want.

"Zen Zone"

A good self-care practice is retreating to your "Zen Zone" if you are feeling difficult emotions. A "Zen Zone" is a safe space that you create for yourself. This space will have everything you need to help you become calm or give yourself time to understand what you are feeling.

Ask your parent/guardian to help you set up a "Zen Zone." You can hang up a "Feelings Chart" and keep fidget toys, art supplies, or a journal in this area as well.

Sometimes, it might be hard to come up with words when dealing with difficult emotions. When this happens, let your parent/guardian know that you would like to go to your "Zen Zone."

Connecting With Others

Healthy and positive relationships are not just an important part of life, but they are also good for your mental well-being. This doesn't mean that you have to be around others *all* the time; it just means that regular, *face-to-face* contact with family, friends, and peers is good for you.

Connecting with others can include hanging out with friends, a walk around the block with your parents, or eating dinner with your family. Establishing these connections can also help you learn to communicate better about your needs and wants, especially when you are experiencing challenging emotions. Limiting social media and spending quality time with your family and friends instead is an important self-care practice for your mental health.

Healthy Diet, Exercise, and Sleep Schedule

Eating healthy, exercising, and getting enough sleep are all very important and contribute to your mental health. For example, eating a lot of sugar may give you a momentary boost, but the crash will leave you feeling groggy and irritable; not getting enough sleep makes it hard to focus and can make you feel cranky or sad.

Physical health and mental health are equally important. You cannot have one without the other, meaning that taking care of your body can help your mind feel better.

Counseling

Your parents can also help you stay on track with good self-care practices. However, they may not be equipped with all the information or resources you need to keep your mind and body healthy. In this case, it's recommended to seek out a professional to help you work through difficult emotions or situations.

For example, if you broke your leg, your parent or guardian would take you to see a doctor or healthcare provider. Similarly, if your emotions, thoughts, or moods become too difficult to deal with on your own, speaking with a mental health professional or a school counselor can help.

ASKING FOR HELP WHEN NEEDED

It can be hard to take care of your mental health on your own. One of the best things you can do, even if you just need help putting your emotions into words, is talking with a trusted adult.

Speak to a trusted adult.

If your emotions and thoughts feel like too much to handle on your own, it is important that you reach out to a trusted adult. Even if you do not completely understand what you are feeling or why you are feeling that way, speaking to someone can help you understand or at least identify what you are feeling.

You may need some time by yourself, perhaps in your "Zen Zone," before you feel calm enough to speak to an adult. There is nothing wrong with waiting to talk to someone about difficult emotions or thoughts. A trusted adult may even be able to tell that something is bothering you without you even mentioning it. They may notice the following signs that you are having a hard time:

- You are very irritable or have emotional outbursts.
- You are withdrawn.
- You've been having trouble in school.
- You have trouble sleeping.
- You purposely hurt yourself or have thoughts about hurting yourself or others.

If you or your family just experienced a difficult situation, such as a death in the family or divorce, they may pay more attention to your behavior and body language. If they notice changes, they may even start the conversation about what you are feeling first.

Even adults have a hard time with strong emotions and thoughts. If your parents or guardians are struggling, they may not be able to give you the help you need in starting self-care practices or helping you feel better. Seeking out a mental health professional can help you and your parents/guardians manage your emotions, thoughts, and moods. This may be a necessary step if your moods, thoughts, or behaviors are signs of a disorder, and not just part of a phase.

A disorder is when your thoughts, moods, or emotions seem out of control and make it difficult for you to live your day-to-day life. The most common disorders among children are anxiety disorders, ADHD (Attention-deficit/hyperactivity disorder), eating disorders, depression, and autism.

Some kids may also experience intense feelings of gender dysphoria when their assigned gender does not match what they feel. These kids will require the attention and care of a mental health professional who is trained to work with someone who experiences gender dysphoria.

There is nothing wrong with having one or more of these disorders; studies show that about 20% of adolescents have been diagnosed with some form of mental disorder. The only way to be sure if you have a disorder is to see a mental health professional who works with children, and he or she will be able to give you the care you need to help you manage the symptoms.

Seek Out a Professional

Finding the right mental health professional takes some time and research. There are different types of professionals who work with children and preteens. For example, a social worker makes sure that you are doing well at home and at school, checking in on you and talking to your caregivers.

Mental health professionals, on the other hand, are often called therapists. While there are different types of therapists, their main goal is to help you understand your emotions and offer ways to help you cope with them better.

All types of therapists will talk to you about your feelings and what is happening in your life. They will help you figure out the best practices that will improve your mental health, and some of them will prescribe medicine to treat your disorder.

Counselors

Counselors work with children and families, and when you go see one, expect them to ask you questions about your feelings, thoughts, behavior, and relationships. They will usually see you one-on-one, and they will try to create a safe space where you can feel comfortable talking to them about whatever is on your mind.

Most schools have on-site counselors trained to provide support to make sure that you do well in school. They may not be trained to deal with mental health issues, but they can direct you and your family to a mental health professional who can help.

Psychologists

Psychologists are experts on human behavior. Some are trained to work with people, adults, and kids who have mental disorders. Many schools will have on-site psychologists who work with children and young people. They also work with teachers, principals, and families to come up with a plan for helping kids who need special attention.

If you are struggling in school, whether it's with your grades or socially, the school psychologist can help you. They may want to speak with your parents or guardian to better understand what you are struggling with, but their goal is to improve your emotional health and attitude. They can also help you deal with anxiety, conflicts that you may have with your peers, or anything else that makes it hard for you to do well at school or at home.

Psychiatrists

Psychiatrists are medical doctors who treat mental health disorders, and they can prescribe medicine to people who need it. While some psychologists can prescribe medicine to treat mental health disorders, it is usually psychiatrists who do this.

98

CHAPTER NINE: LOVE YOURSELF FOR WHO YOU ARE

Making the right choices for yourself as you get older requires you to develop several skills and habits. One of those habits is loving and accepting yourself, which means you must choose to be healthy and surround yourself with positive influences.

An important part of loving and accepting yourself is learning how to navigate the body image issues that you will encounter throughout your life. "Body image" refers to the way you feel about the shape of your body and how it looks. First and foremost, it's important to understand how and why body image plays an important role in the decisions you make yourself.

UNDERSTANDING BODY IMAGE

As your body grows and develops, your physical appearance will become more important to you. It's important to maintain a positive body image for your overall well-being.

However, your body image may be one of the most challenging issues you face while growing up, as you will feel pressured to look a certain way. While it is normal for everyone to have some issues with their body image, it is important to understand the role it plays in your development.

What is body image?

Body image is the way that you think of and how you look at your body. Do you feel perfectly happy with the way you look? Are there parts of your body that you wish you could change?

It's normal for everyone to want to change some parts of their bodies. You may feel unhappy about your teeth, weight, hair, or eyes. However, focusing too much on what you don't like about your body can be bad for your physical and mental health.

There's nothing wrong with wanting to dye your hair, dabbling with makeup, or maintaining a healthy weight. Enhancing your appearance is a healthy choice if you are doing it because you want to or because you want to express yourself.

In some cases, girls with a very negative body image can develop harmful habits, such as an eating disorder. For example, skipping meals or making yourself vomit after eating can cause serious damage to your body. You can start good habits to help you take care of your body, such as eating a nutritious diet and exercising regularly to help maintain a healthy weight.

However, some people experience gender dysphoria. Imagine having a feeling that you were born in the wrong body. In your mind, the way your body looks or may look as you enter puberty does not match the gender that you identify with. For example, an AFAB person may feel extreme distress, anxiety, or depression about developing breasts.

A person with gender dysphoria needs special resources to manage their condition, which is clinical in nature and needs to be addressed with therapy, counseling, and possibly medication.

How does body image affect you?

A negative body image can cause you to develop harmful habits, impacting your physical and mental health. If you are focused on your weight or becoming fat, you might decide to make changes to your diet. While this can be healthy, make sure you make the right decisions. For example, eating healthy portions of nutritious foods, avoiding junk food, and exercising are all healthy choices. On the other hand, skipping meals, over-exercising, or taking diet pills can be harmful to you.

A negative body image can also affect other aspects of your life. If you are unhappy with your weight or body shape, you might feel too embarrassed to go out with your friends. You may even feel too self-conscious to participate in activities that are healthy for your body, such as swimming, dancing, or playing sports.

Becoming preoccupied with how your body looks can lead you to ignore your positive qualities. If all you care about is looking perfect or having the perfect body, you may end up ignoring the skills and qualities that you need to grow into a healthy and happy adult. These can include having a growth mindset, being kind, learning, or being assertive – all of which are important for navigating the world.

Similarly, to how your thoughts and feelings will influence the way you live your life, so does your body image. A negative body image can lead to harmful habits and result in unhealthy effects on every part of your life. When negative thoughts about your body take up a lot of space in your head, it is hard to make room to focus on healthy things that you care about and enjoy.

How does the media affect body image?

There are many factors that can affect your body image, including your beliefs, family, and friends. However, one of the most major – and often problematic – influences on body image is the media. This includes TV shows, movies, music, billboards, magazines, the news, and basically everything you find on the internet, including social media sites.

There are definitely good aspects to the media, as this is where you get information about what is happening in the world and ideas. The media also shows what is "trendy" and "fashionable" at the time while helping you discover ideas, music, art, and information that you have not encountered before.

However, the media can also communicate ideas about what is considered beautiful, attractive, normal, or cool. You may notice that, sometimes, only certain types of faces and bodies are being represented. For example, if you only see thin actresses with long, straight hair and light skin in popular movies and TV shows, this can communicate that those traits are considered beautiful; thankfully, that has been changing. There is increasing diversity in the types of people represented in shows and movies.

It is likely that social media has a stronger influence on body image than movies and TV shows. Almost every kid aged 8 to 12 years old has access to the internet or even a smartphone. Many kids also have access to social media apps, where they connect with friends, follow updates of famous people, and post and share images.

Social media can have a strong influence on children and pre-teens because of peer pressure. Your friends and peers are probably posting pictures and sharing videos and clips of what they find cool and interesting. However, these images may try to show you how to look attractive or cool. Certain looks, body types, or clothes are presented as "perfect."

Friends and peers are an important part of a healthy and happy life, and they have the potential to be a great influence in your life. They can inspire you to be the best version of yourself. You may be asking yourself, "Why shouldn't I pay attention to what they do in school and on social media?"

This is because not all media content helps you feel good about yourself. Social media does not mirror real life, but it may feel like it does.

Why a positive body image is important.

A positive body image is important for several reasons. For one, it is one of the foundations you need for an overall sense of well-being. Another reason why a positive body image is important is because it helps you feel confident in making the right choices for yourself. It empowers you to stand up for your values. You might be more inclined to cave into peer pressure when you have a negative body image and do not feel confident enough to stand up for what is right.

Struggling with body image is not unique to pre-teens; many adults struggle with their body image as well. This is why it's so important to develop healthy habits from a young age.

Healthy habits are important.

Healthy habits are necessary for all people, especially girls entering puberty. Some of these habits include adequate nutrition, a regular sleep schedule, and physical exercise. It is also important to cultivate a positive body image, which means you are embracing these healthy habits and practicing self-care. Self-care isn't just about taking bubble baths or getting manicures; it also involves setting physical, emotional, and mental boundaries and maintaining healthy relationships.

INCREASING BODY POSITIVITY

There are many ways in which you can start to feel positive about your body. Here are a few practices that you can start now and follow throughout your life.

Be comfortable in your body.

One of the most important ways to develop and maintain a positive body image is to be comfortable in your body. While your body and appearance will change throughout your life, it's important to accept your body at every stage and take good care of it.

Being comfortable in your body means:

- Being kind to yourself – no negative self-talk!
- Appreciating your body as it is – genetics influences your size and shape.
- Staying away from trendy diets – exercise and eat nutritious foods instead.
- Focusing on qualities not related to your appearance.
- Wearing clothes that help you feel good.

However, being comfortable in your body can be very difficult for someone with gender dysphoria. This is when counselors and healthcare professionals need to step in.

If you are experiencing feelings of gender dysphoria, you should speak to a trusted adult and ask them to connect you with a mental health professional to get the care that you need.

Appreciate Your Uniqueness

Everyone has unique strengths, abilities, and qualities. An important part of having a positive body image is recognizing what you're good at, what you'd like to get better at, and where your interests lie.

No one is like you. There are qualities that make you different, and only focusing on your looks can cause you to lose sight of what makes you unique. Remember, you do not need to have "perfect" looks to lead a happy life. Family and friends who genuinely respect and admire you can see your uniqueness.

Positive Self-Talk

A good habit that can help you feel better about your body is positive self-talk. Self-talk is when you are speaking to yourself as though you are talking to someone else, something that almost everyone does subconsciously.

Positive self-talk is when you say encouraging and helpful statements to yourself, in your head, or out loud. Even if you're struggling with getting better at math or being nicer to your siblings, you can encourage yourself to get better at those things through positive self-talk. This habit is also important for your body image; instead of pointing out everything you don't like about your body, try telling yourself what you *do* like about your body.

Everyone has room for improvement. Whether you want to get better at gymnastics or wish you could play chess like a grandmaster, there's nothing wrong with wanting to get better *at* something. However, not being great at something – yet – doesn't mean that you are a lousy or stupid person.

Positive Influences

The people around you will influence how you think and act, whether you know it or not. Healthy relationships are important, positive forces in your life. A positive influence encourages you to make choices that are healthy and right for you. They can also inspire you to be the best version of yourself.

People who are positive influences do not pressure you to do anything that compromises your values or is at odds with who you want to be. These influences do not tell you that you need to change the way you look to fit in or be accepted, and they certainly won't be mean to you because of how you look.

Self-Care

Taking care of your mental and physical health is another way to feel positive about your body. Self-care means taking care of yourself by eating a nutritious diet, getting exercise, having a regular sleep schedule, and taking breaks when you need it.

However, self-care also applies to your mental health. Journaling, creating art, and meditating are all good examples of self-care. These activities allow you to express yourself or take the time to slow down a bit during your day. Self-care can improve your mood and how you feel about yourself.

REPAIRING A NEGATIVE BODY IMAGE

Healthy habits, such as positive self-talk, can help you feel good about your body. It is also important to know more strategies for dealing with a negative body image. A negative body image can have a bad effect on your health and wellbeing, making you not want to take good care of yourself.

Challenge Negative Thoughts

Challenging negative thoughts can be difficult to deal with at your age. You are growing, your life is changing, and you're becoming more aware of your body and the world around you. You may get a barrage of messages from your peers, culture, or media about how you should look and act. These messages can make you feel like you are not beautiful or smart enough. Thankfully, there are many ways you can challenge negative thoughts:

- Practice positive self-talk (even writing it down can be helpful).

- Replace negative thoughts with positive thoughts (you can write them out or talk about them).

- List things that you are thankful for.

- Surround yourself with supportive people.

Writing or talking about your negative thoughts can help you figure out what triggered them in the first place. Sometimes, just writing them down or talking about them can help you feel better. However, if you find it difficult to write or talk about your

108

negative thoughts, there are other ways you can communicate them. For example, you can wear a rubber band and gently snap it when you are having a negative thought or feeling. Doing this can let your parent or guardian know what you are feeling.

Sometimes, you can just distract yourself. Dance, go for a walk, or draw to keep your mind focused on something else.

Focus on your good qualities.

Switching your negative thoughts with positive thoughts about yourself is one good way to deal with harmful thoughts and feelings. There are several activities and habits that can help you do this. For example, you can:

- Write a list of your accomplishments.
- Write a list of what you want to achieve in the future.
- Ask trusted family and friends what they like about you.
- Ask trusted family and friends why they enjoy having you around.

Limit your time on social media.

Social media, and the media in general, can have a big influence on how you feel about yourself and your body. While it can be a great tool for connecting with others and getting information, social media can have a negative effect on your self-image and self-esteem. Try limiting your social media usage and be more selective about what you watch, follow, or read. You can ask a trusted adult to help you with this.

Talk to someone.

Healthy relationships are good for your mental and physical health. For that reason, talking to a trusted adult about your thoughts and feelings can be very helpful; it can also help you connect with them. Puberty can be an especially difficult time emotionally, and an adult has probably experienced many of the challenges you are facing.

Your parent/guardian may not have all the information you need, and that's perfectly fine. This is an opportunity to learn together. You can reach out to your school counselor or a professional who can guide you and your parent/guardian to the information and resources you need.

CHAPTER TEN: DEALING WITH PEER PRESSURE

Puberty can be a challenging time, both emotionally and socially. Surrounding yourself with people who care about and support you can help you navigate the changes you will experience. After all, your friends and peers are a core part of your experience.

However, your peers can be a positive or negative influence in your life. Learning how to deal with both types of peer pressure is an important skill to learn.

UNDERSTANDING PEER PRESSURE

In order to effectively handle peer pressure, you should understand what it is and the effect it can have on your life. Sometimes, you may not even be aware of how much your peers are influencing your behavior.

What is peer pressure?

Your peers are kids who are around your age, such as your friends. However, not all your peers are your friends. Try to think about all the kids at your school or in your neighborhood who are close to your age. They're all your peers, and even though not all of them are your friends, they can still influence your thoughts and behavior. This is called peer influence, and it can be good or bad.

Peer influence can be strong. Your peers can influence you through their words, choices, and behavior. Peer pressure is how your friends and peers can influence your behavior. Sometimes this influence can feel like something pressing down on you and making you do something that you wouldn't normally do. There are both positive and negative types of peer pressure.

Knowing how to handle peer pressure can be challenging because you want to feel accepted by your peers. You may feel as if the only way to be accepted by them is to go along with whatever they want to do, but that's not always the case.

Positive and Negative Peer Pressure

Positive peer pressure can influence your choices and behavior in a way that is beneficial to you. Examples of positive peer pressure between you and your peers include:

- Encouraging each other to do well in school.

- Standing up for each other

- Helping each other with self-care habits

Positive peer pressure can inspire you to face your fears or take on challenges that help you achieve your goals, like participating in a dance competition or trying out a new food. This type of pressure can help you stick up for yourself and your values, especially when you are in a challenging situation.

Negative peer pressure, on the other hand, encourages you to do things that are harmful or not aligned with your values. Examples of negative peer pressure include:

- Skipping school because your friends do it.

- Publicly making fun of or picking on another kid because everyone else does

- Wearing clothes that make you feel uncomfortable just because everyone else does.

Keep in mind that this is not a complete list of negative peer pressure, and the consequences of giving in to negative peer pressure won't be the same every time. Even if negative pressure does not directly harm you, it can still make you feel bad.

Effects of Peer Pressure

Positive peer pressure can be a boon to your confidence, mental health, and self-esteem. This type of pressure can inspire you to try new things and go outside your comfort zone, helping you grow as a person. If you have a positive and healthy relationship with your friends, they can encourage you to stand up for yourself and for your values.

Negative peer pressure only makes your life difficult. It can make you less confident and less independent. Over time, you may feel that you will lose the approval of your friends if you do not follow along with their choices. It can be very challenging if your friends are pressuring you to do something that makes you uncomfortable or feels wrong. If they threaten to make fun of you or exclude you, it can be hard to stand up to them.

If your friends pressure you to skip school or take drugs, then you should ask yourself if they are really good friends to keep around. You may be dealing with a lot of peer pressure if you feel hopeless, sad, or angry for a long time. If that's happening, you should start thinking about whether you should break away from those friendships.

Negative peer pressure can lead to bad grades and problems like depression, and it can also make it difficult for you to have healthy relationships with your family and friends.

RESISTING PEER PRESSURE

Resisting peer pressure is an important skill to obtain as you enter adolescence. Below are some basic tips you can follow for pushing back against peer pressure.

Trust Your Instincts

If something doesn't feel right to you, don't ignore your feelings. This is called trusting your instincts. Even if your friends or peers seem to be fine with it, you should go with your thoughts and feelings. Your instincts can help you detect and avoid danger.

If you don't feel comfortable speaking up, you should contact your parent/guardian or reach out to an adult you trust. You should be able to share your feelings with your friends and peers.

Know Your Values

Something can feel wrong if it goes against your beliefs or values. For example, if your friends are gossiping or teasing another kid because their family is from another country, it will feel wrong because you accept and respect people from different backgrounds. If your friends are shoplifting or taking things from stores without paying, it will feel wrong because you believe that taking things that don't belong to you is wrong. Your values are important because they guide your choices and behavior.

Set Firm Boundaries

Your personal, emotional, and mental boundaries are there to protect you from harm. They are also a way to exercise your ability to make choices about your life and body. Knowing what your boundaries are can help you push back against negative peer pressure.

If you are being pressured to do something that crosses one of your boundaries, you'll have a good idea why it feels wrong. It's important to have conversations about boundaries with your family and friends. They can help you set boundaries and discuss ways you can stick to them, even if you find yourself in a difficult situation.

Be Assertive

Even if you know what your values and boundaries are, it can be hard to stand up for yourself. Being able to do this and say "no" is being assertive. Here's what practicing assertiveness can look like:

- Saying "no"
- Initiating or ending conversations
- Asking for things or making requests
- Sharing how you feel about something.

Practicing assertiveness can allow you to pull yourself out of situations that make you feel uncomfortable. It can also give you a sense of control. However, being assertive can be difficult, and standing up to peer pressure can feel uncomfortable or scary. You may fear that you will ruin your friendships, but you have to ask yourself, "Would a real friend pressure me to do something that I feel is wrong?"

Surround yourself with positive friends.

"Friends" who try to pressure you to do things you do not want to do can make you feel bad about yourself. This is why it's so important to surround yourself with friends who care about your well-being and happiness. Positive and supportive friends can help you make the right choices and explore activities or habits that are great for you.

Good friends will help you stick to your values and the boundaries that keep you healthy. They can also give you opportunities to have a say in making plans for how to spend your time.

Speak to a trusted adult.

Learning to make the right choices and standing up for yourself can be hard if you try to do it alone. One of the best ways to deal with peer pressure is to speak to a trusted adult who can give you some advice. You can ask them about:

- Boundaries
- Values
- Saying "no" to negative peer pressure
- Qualities to look for in a friend.

This trusted adult can be someone in your family, community, or at school. If dealing with peer pressure has been hard, you can reach out to your school counselor. They can give you more information and resources.

117

BUILDING A SUPPORT SYSTEM

Dealing with peer pressure can be an overwhelming challenge throughout your adolescence. One of your best defenses against negative peer pressure is a support system of friends and family. As you grow into an adult, you will become more and more independent. You'll learn how to make your own choices about your body, what you do with your time, and the kind of life you would like to live as you reach adulthood.

You can also learn how to deal with difficult situations. Oftentimes, these situations will involve other people. Learning to be independent means being able to stand up for yourself, trusting your instincts, and setting boundaries.

Building a support system of friends and family can help you through the challenges that you will face in your teen years, and even adulthood.

Choose people who care.

People who care about your well-being can help you make healthy choices. This is especially important when it comes to your circle of friends. Positive and supportive friends can help you get through the tough times, respecting your boundaries and rarely pressuring you to do something you do not want to do.

An important thing to keep in mind is that, when it comes to friends, it's quality over quantity. Having even one or two positive, caring friends who have your best interests at heart will help you feel important and valuable.

Share your feelings.

Being able to share your feelings, without being embarrassed, is a necessary part of a healthy and positive relationship. You should be able to share your feelings with close friends; good friends will listen, without making fun of you or making you feel bad about what you are sharing.

Sharing your feelings can also be a way to assert yourself in a conversation. If you are comfortable sharing your feelings with your family, you can learn to be outspoken when you are with friends. This is an important way to assert yourself when you are pushing back against negative peer pressure.

Spend quality time together.

Spending quality time with people who care about you can also be a boost for your confidence. This means doing activities that you find enjoyable and meaningful with people who care about you.

Quality time can be especially meaningful if you feel free to share your own ideas or plans about what you would like to do. It's important that you have a say in what you do with your time. Being able to speak your mind when it comes to hobbies and activities gives you some control over how you spend time with your friends.

Quality time is an important component of any positive and healthy relationship. Feeling connected with people you care about is good for your mental health. It reinforces the fact that you are valued and cared for.

Support

Your friends and family can support you through the toughest times, and this support can come in different forms. Support can consist of encouraging or soothing words. It can also be a favor or simply doing something that makes you feel valued and cared for.

What feels like support can be different for every person. Sometimes you might just want someone to listen to what you have to say. Other times, you might want or need a friend to step in to do more. Remember, you will encounter many challenges throughout your adolescence and adulthood, and good advice and support from others will help you get through challenging moments and situations.

There's only so much you can do on your own, especially as a kid or pre-teen; that's why it's so important to have a support system of family and friends by your side.

Guidance

One of the challenges that you will face is how to deal with people who do not respect you, your boundaries, or values. It can also be hard to fit in at different places, even at school.

You may find the adults in your life helpful. They can guide you to make the right choices and show you ways you can become independent. Your peers can guide you as well. Positive peer pressure can guide you to make the right choices and develop good habits.

CHAPTER ELEVEN: PLANNING YOUR FUTURE

Planning your future is another part of growing up. This means coming up with ideas for what you want to do and thinking about the kind of adult you want to be. It may seem like only grown-ups talk about jobs and careers and that you have all the time in the world to come up with a plan for your life; you may also feel like you are too young to think about your future.

The truth is that you have already been thinking about your future; after all, this entire book is about what lies ahead of you! Understanding the basic facts about puberty and learning how to take care of your mental and physical health are ways of planning ahead. This is especially true if puberty hasn't even started for you yet.

Everything you've read about in this book up to this point is about planning for the future. Whenever you think about growing up, you are thinking about the future. In that spirit, this chapter covers another aspect of growing up: career planning.

Education and career planning are only two of the many aspects of planning for your future. Becoming an adult consists of many things, and deciding what you're going to do with your life is one of them.

This sounds like a big task, but don't be overwhelmed! There are a few steps you can take that will help you get started. Remember, you're not on this journey alone. The trusted adults in your life can help you every step of the way. Your role is to explore and come up with big ideas.

The main thing to remember is that you will always be learning, evolving, and changing, which means you'll constantly be learning new things about yourself and what excites you. There are bound to be things that are interesting to you and, on the other hand, things that you find uninteresting or boring.

Here are some things you need to know about planning your future. Remember, it all starts with *you*!

EDUCATION AND CAREER PLANNING

Planning for your continuing education and career is a huge task, but like any task, it can be broken down into different parts. Planning for your future is a bit easier if you do it in steps, accomplishing one goal before moving on to the next.

Explore Your Interests

Growing up means exploring what you like and embracing new interests. This could mean joining a new after-school club or starting a new hobby, such as creative writing or dance.

Your new interests can include anything, from developing a new skill to helping others through community service and organizing events. Exploring new hobbies and interests can benefit you in many ways, such as helping you:

- Learn a new skill.
- Make friends.
- Think about your future goals.
- Boost your confidence and self-esteem.

For example, learning to play chess or edit videos through vlogging can sharpen your critical thinking skills and enhance your creative thinking skills. Learning to create art with colored pencils or watercolor paint can help you develop your creativity and assist with fine motor skills.

There are also more technical skills, such as learning to code. This can prepare for a career in Information Technology (IT), tech, or in any other field that relies on computers. The skills you learn while searching for your passion are talents that you can use for the rest of your life.

Exploring different hobbies and interests is also a great way to make new friends. Whether it's chess club, bike riding, or tabletop games, participating in activities and hobbies with like-minded people is a great way to learn about yourself, too.

Hobbies can also help build your self-esteem and confidence. Solving puzzles, creating art, or journaling can help you relax and become more confident in your skills and knowledge when you make progress.

Last but not least, exploring hobbies and interests can help you plan for your future. If you start learning a foreign language and enjoy it, this opens many possibilities for you. Some people who love learning languages become teachers or pursue a career that involves international travel.

Your hobbies and interests don't have to become a career path, but they can help you figure out what you are good at and what you enjoy doing. They can also be helpful when you start looking for a job. Your hobbies can show what you are good at and that you have some skills that can be applied in the world outside of the classroom.

Your hobbies and interests will likely change over time, and that's okay. You'll notice that your ideas about careers and education will change as well. This just means that you're learning more, both about the world and about your skills, interests, and abilities.

It is okay to pick a career track that isn't related to one of your hobbies but is attractive to you because you think it will help you make a lot of money. As an adult, you will need money to pay for your food, housing, and everything else. A job can also help you pay for hobbies and interests.

Dream Big

"What do you want to be when you grow up?" is probably a question you have been hearing quite a bit lately. Your answer has probably changed a lot since you were younger, too. This is a good thing, because your interests, hobbies, and passions have most likely changed as well. They will likely keep changing as you get older; even grown-ups take up new hobbies and change careers sometimes!

An important part of planning your career or education is to dream big. Are there jobs that you think are cool? What kinds of things would you like to do as you get older? In asking yourself these questions, you use your imagination to dream up what your life can look like when you are all grown up.

It's great to be excited about what you can do when you become an adult. However, a job or career doesn't only have to be about paying for things you need. It can also be something you love doing that you just so happen to get paid for.

Your values and beliefs will also help shape your dreams about the future. You might be passionate about the environment or feel strongly that all children deserve a good education. In this case, you can become an activist or advocate for those who do not have access to clean water or a quality education.

Talk to adults.

Almost any adult you'll talk to has or has had a job. They may be able to answer questions you have about what it's like to do the kind of work they do and why they have chosen their job. Be prepared to get different answers.

Another great way to learn about what it's like having a certain job is to participate in a "Take Your Child to Work" day. On this special day, your parent or mentor can take you to work with them. You will see and learn about what they do at work firsthand, and you will also see other kinds of jobs that the people around them do. The trusted adults in your life can give you some ideas or help as you explore your interests by guiding you in the right direction.

Speak to a school counselor and attend career days.

School counselors play a special role in career planning and education. Not only do they help you do your best in school, but they can also help you figure out what you want to do in your life as an adult.

Your school counselor can give you books and information on different career paths, as well as other aspects of being an adult.

They can also give you a list of people that you can talk to about career choices. Additionally, your school counselor may work with teachers and parents to plan special career days at school. A career day usually involves real-life professionals visiting your school to talk about what they do. It can also include asking students to do research on a specific profession or career.

Other career day activities can include:

- Creating your first resume
- Doing a research poster on a career that interests you.
- Interviewing your parents and neighbors about their jobs.

Many schools will host a career day. If your school does not plan one, you can talk to your teacher or school counselor about starting one.

Do some research.

The internet truly opens the world to you, giving you access to all the information and knowledge that you want with just a few clicks. You can read articles and watch videos about different colleges and careers. A trusted adult can help you navigate the internet to find the most helpful sources.

The librarian at your school or neighborhood library can also help you find books on careers and jobs in fields that are interesting to you. This is also a good way to explore career possibilities that you have never imagined. Your teacher, parents, and mentors can also help answer questions you have about careers that interest you.

Networking

A computer network connects websites all over the world. It is through a network that you get information, and it allows you to communicate, shop, read, and watch videos. A computer network can help you connect with other people from around the world.

A network of people, including family, friends, and mentors, works in much the same way an electronic one does. Your network can connect you to different opportunities and professionals who will allow you to explore your interests and passions.

Networking is an important part of career planning because having the right skills and experience isn't always enough to help you get a job. It's good to know people who are part of a professional network because they can introduce you to new people and vouch for you. However, a network isn't just about meeting professionals. Your network also includes people who are an important part of your daily life, such as family, friends, and teachers. They care about your well-being and happiness, and they want you to succeed in life.

PLANNING YOUR FUTURE

Deciding what you want to do with your life is a huge task and may seem overwhelming. The important thing to keep in mind is that big projects and tasks can be broken up into smaller steps and goals. Breaking up an important project, like planning for the

128

future, into smaller parts can make big goals easier to achieve. Doing this can also build your confidence in your skills and knowledge.

Plotting out smaller steps and goals also allows you to make changes when necessary. Keep in mind that no one can predict the future, and even if you follow all the steps, there's no guarantee that you'll end up where you planned.

Your interests will change over time. As you get older, you'll learn more about yourself and the world around you. Planning for your future by creating and achieving smaller goals will allow you to change your plans when you need to.

Checklists

Typing up a checklist is a helpful way of setting up and keeping track of your goals. Remember, break up big tasks into smaller ones! You can jot down your goals for the week, a couple of months, or even for the year. Think about what you want your life to look like a year from now. Here are some exercises and questions to get you thinking about your goals:

- What do you think you need to do to make it happen?

- Who can you talk to that can help achieve it?

- How will you keep track of your goals?

These are just a few examples of questions you can ask yourself when coming up with your list of goals. The simplest way to keep track of them is to write them down or use an app. You can also create a collage of pictures, art, or anything else that encourages you and reminds you of your goals. Your imagination is the only limit.

If you feel stuck in coming up with anything, you can ask a trusted adult, such as a school counselor, parent, or mentor, to help you.

Learning Important Skills

In order to reach your goals, you'll need to be willing to learn along the way. There are some skills that you'll need to keep developing, such as reading, writing, and speaking. This is because knowing how to communicate well is important in many parts of your life, including your career.

Problem-solving is also an important part of growing up, and this skill is an important feature in practically every job. Another important skill is cooperation. Whether you are working on a group project, are part of a dance troupe, or simply playing with your friends, you are working as part of a team. Some of your goals will require you to work with others.

Finally, it's vitally important to learn about money. Many goals can take up a lot of time, and sometimes they require money, too. Understanding money includes knowing the costs of activities and equipment, such as the cost of dance lessons or musical instruments.

Research

In order to set realistic goals and plans for yourself, you need to understand what it is that you would like to achieve. For example, if you want to become a famous pianist when you grow up, what steps are required to get there? Finding the answers to these questions means doing research to discover important information, such as:

- The skills and training you need.

- What schools or professional organizations you need to join

- The materials and equipment you need

- Who you need to contact

A career in any field requires that you take certain steps, such as doing well at school, going to college, and getting a degree in a relevant field. Even if your dream is to become an online content creator, you'll still need to do research. Becoming a content creator takes time, effort, and information. You can find a lot of information online or at your school and local library.

Your school counselor can also help you explore your career interests. They may even be able to help you develop a plan and recommend materials that you and your parents, guardian, or mentor can read together.

BALANCING SCHOOL AND HOBBIES

Setting goals and planning for your future means that you will be very busy. It's important that you learn how to balance school and hobbies with other parts of your life. Below are a few tips that you can take advantage of.

Time Management

Time management is a skill that allows you to balance school with your extra-curricular activities. Striking a balance is important for achieving your goals and plans but is especially important for your physical and mental health. This is because a busy schedule can cause you to lose out on sleep or neglect your health. If this is the case, you may have to cut back on some activities or commitments.

As a pre-teen, it's important to prioritize sleep, meals, and school. Mastering time-management skills allows you to make time for both academics and your hobbies instead of giving up a good sleep schedule or quality time with friends and family.

Self-Care

Taking care of your physical and mental health should *always* be a priority. This means that sometimes your goals may take a back seat. You won't be able to achieve your goals, big or small if you're sick or burned out all the time. Don't forget to:

- Get enough sleep
- Eat a nutritious diet
- Drink plenty of water
- Exercise

Getting Help

It's important to remember, through all this planning, that you're still a kid. A trusted adult will sometimes need to step in and help you. You may need help figuring out your goals, keeping track of them, or staying healthy and taking care of yourself properly.

You are not alone. Don't be shy about asking for help! Speaking to a trusted adult can help you in many ways, even if you just need them to listen as you share your feelings and struggles.

134

CONCLUSION

Hopefully, growing up feels less daunting and scary now. You should have a better understanding of the changes that you might have begun to experience.

Puberty is just one part of growing up, but it's an important one. The changes you'll experience are physical, mental, and emotional. Menstruation and breasts are just two physical changes that AFAB people can expect. While you and your peers will go through these physical changes, there is no need to compare. Everyone develops at their own pace.

If you have lingering questions about your body and puberty, a healthcare professional can give you more information and guidance. This book could have just focused on puberty; however, as you learned, there's a lot more to growing up.

Growing up into a healthy and happy adult means learning how to take care of yourself by developing and maintaining good habits and routines. This includes eating a nutritious diet, exercising, and getting enough sleep. It also includes making yourself feel good, inside *and* out.

Learning how to manage your thoughts, moods, and emotions is another facet of taking care of yourself. Stress and anxiety are a part of everyone's life, but they can get in the way of your mental health if they become unmanageable. Learning how to cope with stress and anxiety is one of the best ways to take care of yourself.

Your relationships with your family and friends will also change during this time. As you learn to become independent and make your own choices about your life, it's important to learn about setting personal boundaries. Boundaries are a way of protecting yourself, and they are physical, emotional, and mental. The most important lesson about boundaries is that they are part of self-care, and you should always communicate to others how you would like to be treated.

Boundaries are a "pillar" of healthy and positive relationships. As a kid, it can be hard to set and maintain your boundaries, so asking a trusted adult to help you is a good idea. It also helps to surround yourself with people who care about and support you.

Along with setting personal boundaries, building positive and healthy relationships is another part of growing up. These relationships can help you get through tough times and are necessary for good physical and mental health. Puberty and adolescence can be a challenging time for many, and it helps to have caring and supportive people in your life.

One of the toughest issues you may face during adolescence is your body image. Remember, body image is how you see yourself. It mainly has to do with how you feel about your body and overall appearance. It can be hard to have a healthy body image if you are always getting messages about what is cool or beautiful. However, it's important to love yourself for who you are. You need to appreciate your unique qualities.

When you want to fit in or be accepted by your peers and friends, you may feel a lot of pressure to look or act in certain ways. This is called peer pressure. It can be positive or negative, and it is important to learn how to recognize the difference.

Positive peer pressure can inspire you to make healthy and positive decisions and can reinforce a positive body image. Your friends and peers can help you learn about the world and your interests.

Negative peer pressure, as you remember from Chapter 10, can make you feel insecure and bad about yourself. This can cause you to make unhealthy decisions, such as skipping school or participating in activities that are harmful to your mental and physical health. Being able to make good choices and maintain your independence when facing negative peer pressure is an important skill.

Resisting negative peer pressure can be very challenging, though. As a kid, you may not be able to do it all on your own. It takes time and effort to feel comfortable enough to stand up for yourself and push back. This is why surrounding yourself with positive and healthy relationships is a part of becoming a healthy and happy adult.

Growing up means thinking and talking about the future. Your values, beliefs, and interests can help you decide what kind of life you want to live and how to achieve your goals. When it comes to growing up, having a career is a big part of life as an adult. After all, becoming independent has a practical component.

Being independent means paying for food, bills, and other necessities. People have jobs because it helps them pay the bills, but that doesn't have to be the only reason why you choose a certain career. Exploring your interests and skills is a good first step to take when starting to plan your career.

Hopefully, you will feel more excited about your future and growing up. Now, you have the basic knowledge needed to embark on your path to adulthood and live out your unique story.

Printed in Great Britain
by Amazon